quick-method
CLASSIC BLUE
QUILTS

**A LEISURE ARTS PUBLICATION
PRESENTED BY OXMOOR HOUSE**

EDITORIAL STAFF

Vice President and Editor-in-Chief:
  Anne Van Wagner Childs
Executive Director: Sandra Graham Case
Editorial Director: Susan Frantz Wiles
Creative Art Director: Gloria Bearden
Senior Graphics Art Director: Melinda Stout

DESIGN
Design Director:
  Patricia Wallenfang Sowers
Senior Designer: Linda Diehl Tiano
Designer: Anne Pulliam Stocks

PRODUCTION
Managing Editor: Kristine Anderson Mertes
Technical Writers:
  Sherry Solida Ford, Diane Gillian Johns,
  Christopher M. McCarty, and
  Barbara McClintock Vechik
Production Assistant: Sharon Heckel Gillam

EDITORIAL
Managing Editor: Linda L. Trimble
Associate Editor: Terri Leming Davidson
Assistant Editors:
  Tammi Williamson Bradley,
  Stacey Robertson Marshall,
  Karen Temple Walker, and
  Janice L. Wojcik
Editorial Assistant: Shannon Zulpo
Copy Editor: Laura Lee Weland

ART
Book/Magazine Graphics Art Director:
  Diane M. Hugo
Graphics Illustrators:
  Wendy Ward Lair and
  M. Katherine Yancey
Photography Stylists: Pam Choate,
  Sondra Daniel, Karen Smart Hall,
  Aurora Huston, and Christina Tiano Myers

BUSINESS STAFF

Publisher: Bruce Akin
Vice President, Marketing: Guy A. Crossley
Vice President and General Manager:
  Thomas L. Carlisle
Retail Sales Director: Richard Tignor
Vice President, Retail Marketing:
  Pam Stebbins

Retail Marketing Director:
  Margaret Sweetin
Retail Customer Services Manager:
  Carolyn Pruss
General Merchandise Manager:
  Russ Barnett
Vice President, Finance: Tom Siebenmorgen
Distribution Director: Rob Thieme

Library of Congress Catalog Number 97-73654
Hardcover ISBN 0-8487-1615-9
Softcover ISBN 1-57486-068-2

INTRODUCTION

The timeless pairing of blue and white is as fresh today as it was generations ago. From the exquisite porcelain of ancient China to the genteel decor of Colonial America, the crisp combination has been the essence of refinement. Naturally, blue and white designs have always held a special place in the hearts of quilters, whose favorite patterns were often highlighted with these peaceful shades in masterful "best quilts." To showcase the ageless appeal of this refreshing color couplet, we present Quick-Method Classic Blue Quilts, *a cool collection of time-honored patterns in soothing shades of navy, indigo, and azure. Tempered with tones of white, our beloved designs are made using today's updated methods, such as rotary cutting, grid-piecing, and other easy techniques. Each comforting quilt and wall hanging is rated by skill level, so you'll know at a glance which projects are right for you. It's also fun to incorporate blue into your decor with a bevy of smaller accessories, including pillows, valances, and embellished sheets. Whether your style is Victorian, country, or eclectic, the following pages are full of ideas that will have you "stitching the blues!"*

TABLE OF CONTENTS

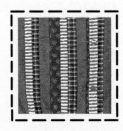

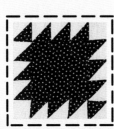

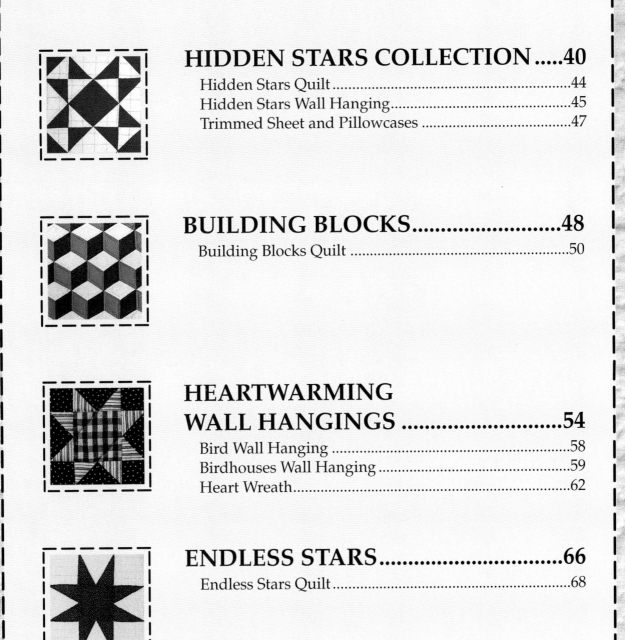

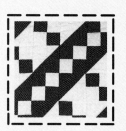

RUFFLED WEDDING RING COLLECTION

This beautiful quilt will be the "something blue" for a young bride in your family. Originating during the Depression, the Double Wedding Ring pattern has become a tradition in quilting, and it continues to be a romantic favorite for today's newlyweds. The interlocking rings of the design — symbolizing the unity of marriage — are formed with a combination of strip-piecing and templates. A lovely floral quilting design enhances the open areas of the quilt and the matching pillow shams. Create a truly memorable gift by including pieces of fabric from the couple's childhood clothing.

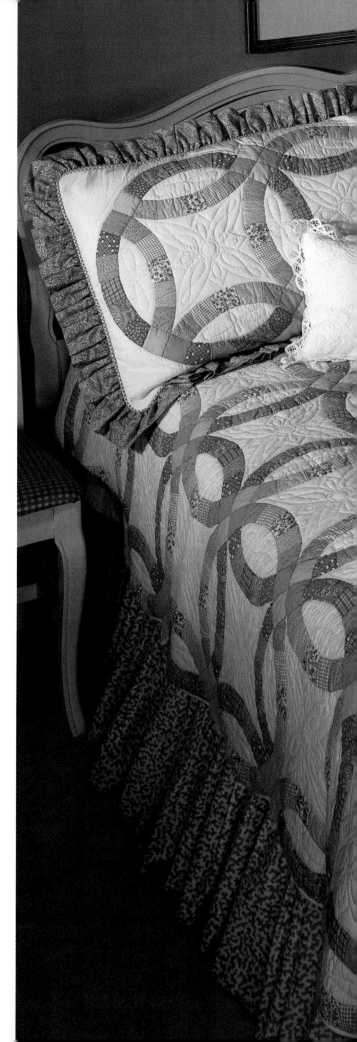

*E*mbroidered with the names of the bride and groom, our Double Wedding Ring album (below) will hold a treasury of wedding-day photos and mementos. Attached to ribbon streamers, tiny decorative wedding rings echo the patchwork design appliquéd on the cover. Custom-made accessories (opposite) coordinate beautifully with our charming quilt. A single Wedding Ring motif is featured on the throw pillow, which is finished with simple welting. Completed with basic grid quilting, the ruffled valance is edged with a scalloped border adapted from the quilt.

DOUBLE WEDDING RING QUILT

SKILL LEVEL: 1 2 3 4 5
RING SIZE: 16½" dia.
QUILT SIZE: 86" x 109"

YARDAGE REQUIREMENTS
Yardage is based on 45"w fabric.

- 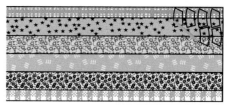 7¾ yds **total** of assorted blue prints
- 6¼ yds of white solid
- ⅝ yd of blue solid
- ⅝ yd of light blue solid
  8 yds for backing
  1 yd for binding
  120" x 120" batting

CUTTING OUT THE PIECES
All measurements include a ¼" seam allowance. Follow Rotary Cutting, page 142, to cut fabric.

1. **From assorted blue prints:**
   - Cut a total of 16 **narrow strips** 3"w.
   - Cut a total of 32 **wide strips** 5"w.

2. **From blue solid:**
   - Cut 8 strips 2"w. From these strips, cut 156 **squares** 2" x 2".

3. **From light blue solid:**
   - Cut 8 strips 2"w. From these strips, cut 156 **squares** 2" x 2".

ASSEMBLING THE STRIP SETS
Follow Piecing and Pressing, page 144, to make strip sets.

1. Beginning and ending with **narrow strips**, sew 2 **narrow** and 4 **wide strips** together in random order to make **Strip Set**. Make 8 **Strip Sets**.

Strip Set (make 8)

TEMPLATE CUTTING
Use patterns, page 18, and follow Template Cutting, page 144, to cut fabric.

1. From **Strip Sets**, use **Template A** to cut 568 **A's** (284 in reverse), positioning center line of template on seam as shown in **Fig. 1**.

Fig. 1

2. From assorted blue prints, use **Template B** to cut 284 **B's**.

3. From white solid, use **Template C** to cut 142 **C's** and **Template D** to cut 63 **D's**.

ASSEMBLING THE QUILT TOP
Follow Piecing and Pressing, page 144, to make quilt top.

1. Sew 1 **A**, 1 **B**, and 1 reverse **A** together to make **Unit 1**. Make 284 **Unit 1's**.

Unit 1 (make 284)

2. Sew 2 blue **squares** and 1 **Unit 1** together to make **Unit 2a**. Make 72 **Unit 2a's**. Sew 2 light blue **squares** and 1 **Unit 1** together to make **Unit 2b**. Make 70 **Unit 2b's**.

Unit 2a (make 72)

Unit 2b (make 70)

3. (*Note:* For curved seams in Steps 3 - 7, match centers and pin at center and at dots, then match and pin between these points. Sew seam with convex edge on bottom next to feed dogs. When joining Units, do not sew into seam allowances; begin and end stitching ¼" from raw edges.) Sew 1 **C** and 1 **Unit 1** together to make **Unit 3**. Make 142 **Unit 3's**.

Unit 3 (make 142)

4. Sew 1 **Unit 2a** and 1 **Unit 3** together to make **Unit 4a**. Make 72 **Unit 4a's**. Sew 1 **Unit 2b** and 1 **Unit 3** together to make **Unit 4b**. Make 70 **Unit 4b's**.

Unit 4a (make 72)    **Unit 4b** (make 70)

5. Matching blue **squares** to light blue **squares**, sew 2 **Unit 4a's**, 2 **Unit 4b's**, and 1 **D** together to make **Unit 5**. Make 32 **Unit 5's**.

Unit 5 (make 32)

6. Sew 1 **Unit 4a** and 1 **D** together to make **Unit 6a**. Make 8 **Unit 6a's**. Sew 1 **Unit 4b** and 1 **D** together to make **Unit 6b**. Make 6 **Unit 6b's**.

Unit 6a (make 8) 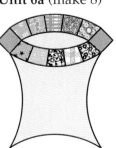   **Unit 6b** (make 6)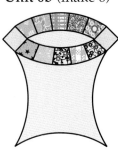

7. Matching blue **squares** to light blue **squares**, follow **Assembly Diagram** to sew **Unit 5's**, **Unit 6a's**, **Unit 6b's** and remaining **D's** together into horizontal rows. Sew rows together.

8. Refer to Steps 2 - 4 of **Working with Diamonds and Set-in Seams**, page 145, and **Assembly Diagram** to sew one **square** at each intersection around outside edge to complete **Quilt Top**.

Assembly Diagram

COMPLETING THE QUILT

1. Follow **Quilting**, page 149, to mark, layer, and quilt, using **Quilting Diagram** as a suggestion. Our quilt is hand quilted.
2. Cut a 33" square of binding fabric. Follow **Making Continuous Bias Strip Binding**, page 153, to make approximately 11 yds of 1¹/₂"w bias binding.
3. Follow Steps 1 and 2 of **Attaching Binding with Mitered Corners**, page 154, to pin binding to front of quilt. Using a ¹/₄" seam allowance, sew binding to quilt, easing curves and leaving a 2" overlap. Trim excess binding and stitch overlap in place. Fold binding over to quilt backing and pin in place, covering stitching line. Blindstitch binding to backing.

Quilting Diagram

PILLOW SHAMS

PILLOW SHAM SIZE: 20" x 30" (without ruffle)

Instructions are for making 2 pillow shams.

YARDAGE REQUIREMENTS
Yardage is based on 45"w fabric.

- 1⁷/₈ yds of assorted blue prints
- 1³/₈ yds of white solid
- 1 fat eighth (9" x 22" piece) of blue solid
- 1 fat eighth (9" x 22" piece) of light blue solid
  2 pieces 21" x 31" for sham top backings
  2 pieces 21" x 31" of batting
  2 pieces 7" x 200" (pieced as necessary) for ruffles
  6¹/₄ yds of ¹/₄" cord for welting
  6¹/₄ yds of 2¹/₂"w bias strip (pieced as necessary) for welting

You will also need:
  transparent monofilament thread for appliqué

CUTTING OUT THE PIECES
All measurements include a ¹/₄" seam allowance unless otherwise specified. Follow Rotary Cutting, page 142, to cut fabric.

1. **From assorted blue prints:**
   - Cut a total of 4 **narrow strips** 3"w.
   - Cut a total of 8 **wide strips** 5"w.
   - Cut 4 pieces 21" x 18¹/₂" for **sham backs**.
2. **From white solid:**
   - Cut 2 **rectangles** 21" x 31" for sham tops.
3. **From blue solid:**
   - Cut 16 **squares** 2" x 2".
4. **From light blue solid:**
   - Cut 16 **squares** 2" x 2".

MAKING THE SHAMS
Follow Piecing and Pressing, page 144, to make pillow shams.

1. Refer to Step 1 of **Assembling the Strip Sets**, page 12, to make 2 **Strip Sets**.
2. Refer to **Template Cutting**, page 12, to cut 56 **A's** (28 in reverse) from **Strip Sets**; 28 **B's** from assorted blue prints; and 14 **C's** and 4 **D's** from white solid.
3. Refer to Steps 1 - 4 of **Assembling the Quilt Top**, page 12, to make 28 **Unit 1's**, 6 **Unit 2a's**, 8 **Unit 2b's**, 14 **Unit 3's**, 6 **Unit 4a's**, and 8 **Unit 4b's**.
4. Matching blue **squares** to light blue **squares**, sew 2 **Unit 4a's**, 2 **Unit 4b's**, and 1 **D** together to make **Unit 5**. Make 2 **Unit 5's**.

Unit 5 (make 2)

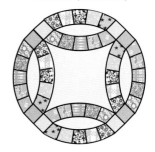

5. Sew 1 **Unit 4a**, 2 **Unit 4b's**, and 1 **D** together to make **Unit 6**. Make 2 **Unit 6's**.

Unit 6 (make 2)

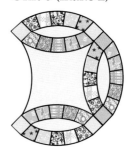

6. Matching blue **squares** to light blue **squares**, follow **Pillow Sham Assembly Diagram** to sew **Unit 5** and **Unit 6** together to make **Unit 7**. Make 2 **Unit 7's**.

Unit 7 (make 2)

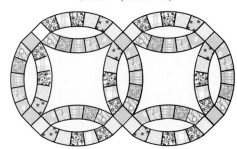

7. Refer to Steps 2 - 4 of **Working with Diamonds and Set-in Seams**, page 145, and **Pillow Sham Assembly Diagram** to sew 1 square each at top and bottom intersections between rings to make **Wedding Ring Appliqué**. Make 2 **Wedding Ring Appliqués**.
8. Press raw edges of each appliqué ¼" to wrong side. Center 1 **Wedding Ring Appliqué** on each **rectangle** and follow **Mock Hand Appliqué**, page 147, to stitch appliqué in place to make **Pillow Sham Tops**.
9. Follow **Quilting**, page 149, to mark, layer, and quilt pillow sham tops, using **Quilting Diagram**, page 14, as a suggestion. Our sham tops are hand quilted.
10. Using a ½" seam allowance, follow **Adding Welting to Pillow Top**, page 155, and **Adding Ruffle to Pillow Top**, page 156, to add welting and ruffle to each sham top.
11. On each sham back piece, press one 21" edge ½" to the wrong side; press ½" to the wrong side again and stitch in place.
12. To make each sham back, place 2 **sham back pieces** right side up. Referring to **Fig. 1**, overlap finished edges and baste in place.

Fig. 1

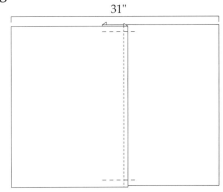

13. To complete each sham, place **sham back** and **Pillow Sham Top** right sides together. Stitch through all layers as close as possible to welting. Cut corners diagonally; remove basting threads. Turn shams right side out; press.

Pillow Sham Assembly Diagram

DOUBLE WEDDING RING THROW PILLOW

Pillow Size: 20" x 20"

SUPPLIES

³/₄ yd **total** of 45"w assorted blue print fabrics
³/₈ yd of 45"w white solid fabric
20" x 20" **large square** of white solid fabric
4 **squares** 2" x 2" of blue solid fabric
4 **squares** 2" x 2" of light blue solid fabric
20" x 20" piece of fabric for pillow top backing
20" x 20" piece of fabric for pillow back
20" x 20" batting
2½ yds of ¼" dia. cord for welting
2½ yds of 2½"w bias strip (pieced as necessary) for welting
polyester fiberfill
transparent monofilament thread for appliqué

MAKING THE PILLOW

*All measurements include a ¼" seam allowance unless otherwise specified. Follow **Piecing and Pressing**, page 144, to make pillow.*

1. From assorted blue print fabrics, cut 2 **narrow strips** 3"w and 4 **wide strips** 5"w. Refer to Step 1 of **Assembling the Strip Sets**, page 12, to make 1 **Strip Set**.
2. Use patterns, page 18, and follow **Template Cutting**, page 12, to cut 16 **A's** (8 in reverse) from **Strip Set**, 8 **B's** from assorted blue prints, and 4 **C's** and 1 **D** from white solid fabric.
3. Refer to Steps 1 - 5 of **Assembling the Quilt Top**, page 12, to make 1 **Unit 5** for ring appliqué. (You will need 8 **Unit 1's**, 2 **Unit 2a's**, 2 **Unit 2b's**, 4 **Unit 3's**, 2 **Unit 4a's**, and 2 **Unit 4b's**.)
4. Press raw edges of ring appliqué ¼" to wrong side. Center appliqué on **large square** and follow **Mock Hand Appliqué**, page 147, to stitch in

place to make **Pillow Top**.

5. Follow **Quilting**, page 149, to mark, layer, and quilt pillow top, using **Quilting Diagram**, page 14, as a suggestion. Our pillow top is hand quilted.

6. Follow **Pillow Finishing**, page 155, to complete pillow with welting.

WEDDING RING VALANCE

SUPPLIES

scraps of assorted print and solid fabrics for border
solid fabric for valance top, valance top backing, and valance lining
batting
$1/4$" dia. cord for welting
$2 1/2$"w bias strip for welting
fabric for ruffle

MEASURING FOR VALANCE

1. (*Note:* A return is the short portion of the curtain rod that bends back toward the wall to hook over the bracket on each side of the window.) To determine width of valance, measure length of rod, including returns (if applicable); add $1/2$".

2. Round measurement up to a number divisible by 13.

3. Divide valance width by 13 to determine number of scallops needed.

MAKING THE VALANCE

*All measurements include a $1/4$" seam allowance unless otherwise specified. Follow **Rotary Cutting**, page 142, to cut fabric. Follow **Piecing and Pressing**, page 144, to make valance.*

1. Cut 2 **narrow strips** 3"w and 4 **wide strips** 5"w from assorted print fabrics. Cut 1 **square** 2" x 2" for each scallop and 1 additional **square** 2" x 2" for end of border from solid fabrics.

2. For valance top, valance top backing, and valance lining, cut 1 rectangle each 15" by the measurement determined in Step 2 of **Measuring for Valance** from solid fabric.

3. Use **strips** cut in Step 1 and refer to Step 1 of **Assembling the Strip Sets**, page 12, to make 1 **Strip Set**.

4. Refer to **Template Cutting**, page 12, to cut 2 **A's** (1 in reverse) from **Strip Set** and 3 **B's** from assorted blue prints for each scallop.

5. Sew 1 **A**, 3 **B's**, 1 reverse **A**, and 1 **square** together to make 1 **scallop**. Make number of scallops determined in Step 3 of **Measuring for Valance**.

scallop

6. Sew **scallops** and remaining **square** end to end to make **border**.

border

7. Mark center of **border** and 1 long edge (bottom) of **valance top**. Press top raw edge of **border** $1/4$" to wrong side. Matching centers, position **border** right side up along lower edge on right side of **valance top**. Follow **Mock Hand Appliqué**, page 147, to stitch **border** to **valance top**, stitching along top edge of **border** only.

8. Follow **Quilting**, page 149, to mark, layer, and quilt valance, using **Quilting Diagram** as a suggestion. Our valance is hand quilted.

9. Trim valance even with bottom edge of border. Trim ends of border even with side edges of valance. Trim batting and backing even with valance top.

10. Multiply valance width, determined in Step 2 of **Measuring For Valance**, by 2. Cut a piece of fabric 7" by the determined measurement (piecing as necessary) for ruffle.

11. (*Note:* Add welting and ruffle along bottom edge of valance only, use valance lining in place of pillow back, and do not stuff valance with fiberfill.) Using a $1/2$" seam allowance, refer to **Pillow Finishing**, page 155, to make valance.

12. For rod pocket, press top edge of valance 1" to wrong side. Press 2" to wrong side; hand stitch in place close to first fold.

Quilting Diagram

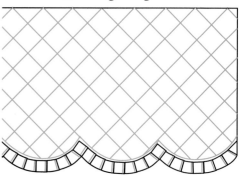

DOUBLE WEDDING RING PHOTO ALBUM

SUPPLIES

1 yd of 45"w white print fabric
scraps of assorted blue print fabrics for appliqué
20" x 30" fabric rectangle for album cover backing
10" x $11 1/2$" x 2" photo album
batting
2 pieces $9 1/2$" x $10 1/2$" of lightweight cardboard
$1/8$"w blue ribbon

¹/₈"w white ribbon
3 ribbon roses
2 decorative rings
embroidery floss
paper-backed fusible web
transparent monofilament thread
transfer paper
removable fabric marking pen
hot glue gun and glue sticks

MAKING THE ALBUM COVER

1. From white print, cut 1 large rectangle 20" x 30" for **album cover** and 2 small rectangles 12" x 13¹/₂" for **inside album covers**. Cut 1 piece of batting 20" x 30".
2. Center open album on right side of **album cover**. Referring to **Fig. 1**, use removable pen to draw around top, bottom, and right edge of album front only (shown in pink). Remove album and use pen to connect top and bottom lines to mark left side of **album cover front** (**Fig. 2**).

Fig. 1

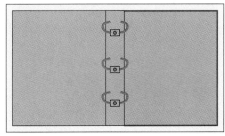

Fig. 2

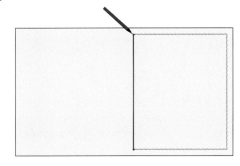

3. Use pattern, page 18, and follow **Preparing Fusible Appliqués**, page 146, to make 22 **ring segments** from assorted blue print scraps. Use pattern, page 19, and transfer paper to transfer **photo album rings** to **album cover front**. Follow manufacturer's instructions to fuse **ring segments** to transferred pattern, overlapping as necessary.
4. Follow **Invisible Appliqué**, page 146, to stitch appliqués to **album cover front**.
5. Use removable pen to write names and date inside rings. Use 3 strands of floss to work **Stem Stitch**, page 157, over drawn lines.
6. Follow **Quilting**, page 149, to mark, layer, and quilt album cover, using **Photo Album Quilting Diagram** as a suggestion.

COVERING THE ALBUM

1. Cut 1 piece of batting 10" x 25". With album closed, glue batting to outside of album.
2. Centering design area on front of album, place open album on wrong side of **album cover**. Leaving 2" around edges of photo album, trim album cover, batting, and backing. Stitching through all layers, baste along edges of album cover.
3. Fold corners of **album cover** diagonally over corners of album; glue in place.
4. Taking care not to distort shape of design area, fold short edges of album cover over side edges of album; glue in place. Fold long edges of album cover over top and bottom edges of album, trimming album cover to fit ¹/₄" under ends of album hardware; glue in place. Remove basting thread.
5. Measure length (top to bottom) of album along hardware; subtract 1". Cut 2 pieces of fabric 2" by the determined measurement. Press short ends of each piece ¹/₄" to wrong side.
6. On inside cover of album, center and glue 1 piece along each side of album hardware with 1 long edge of each piece tucked approximately ¹/₄" under hardware.
7. Center 1 piece of cardboard on wrong side of 1 **inside album cover**. Fold edges of fabric over edges of cardboard; glue in place. Repeat to cover remaining cardboard piece.
8. Center and glue covered cardboard pieces inside front and back covers of album.
9. Tie several lengths of blue and white ribbons into a bow. Tie 1 end of 1 streamer through 1 ring. Repeat for remaining ring. Arrange bow and rings on album front; glue in place. Glue roses over knot in bow.

Photo Album Quilting Diagram

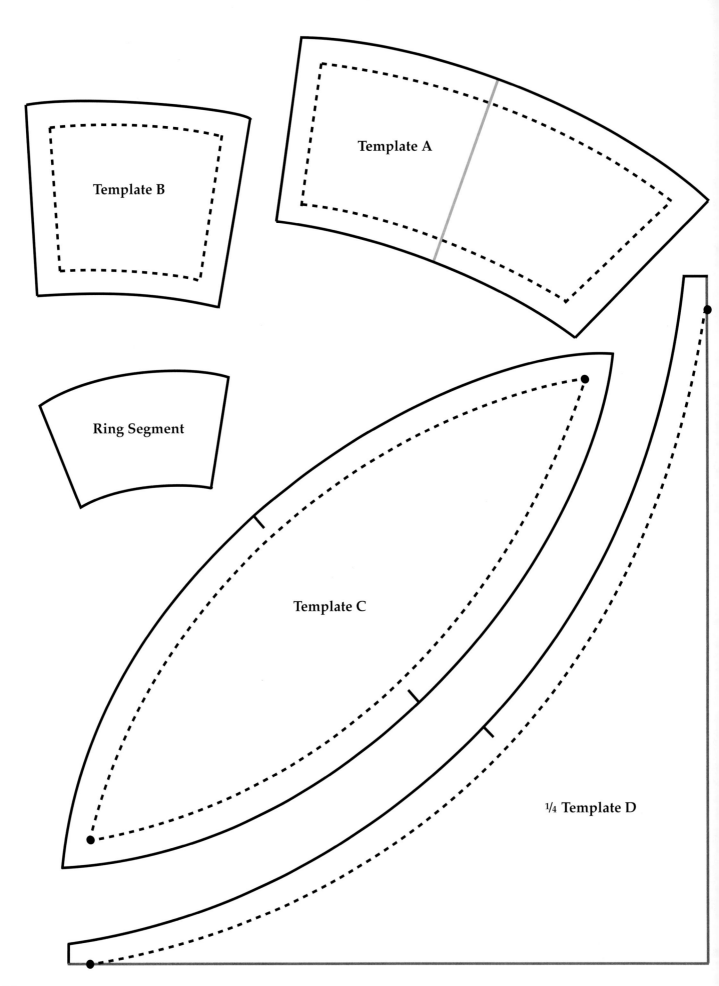

Template B

Template A

Ring Segment

Template C

¼ Template D

18

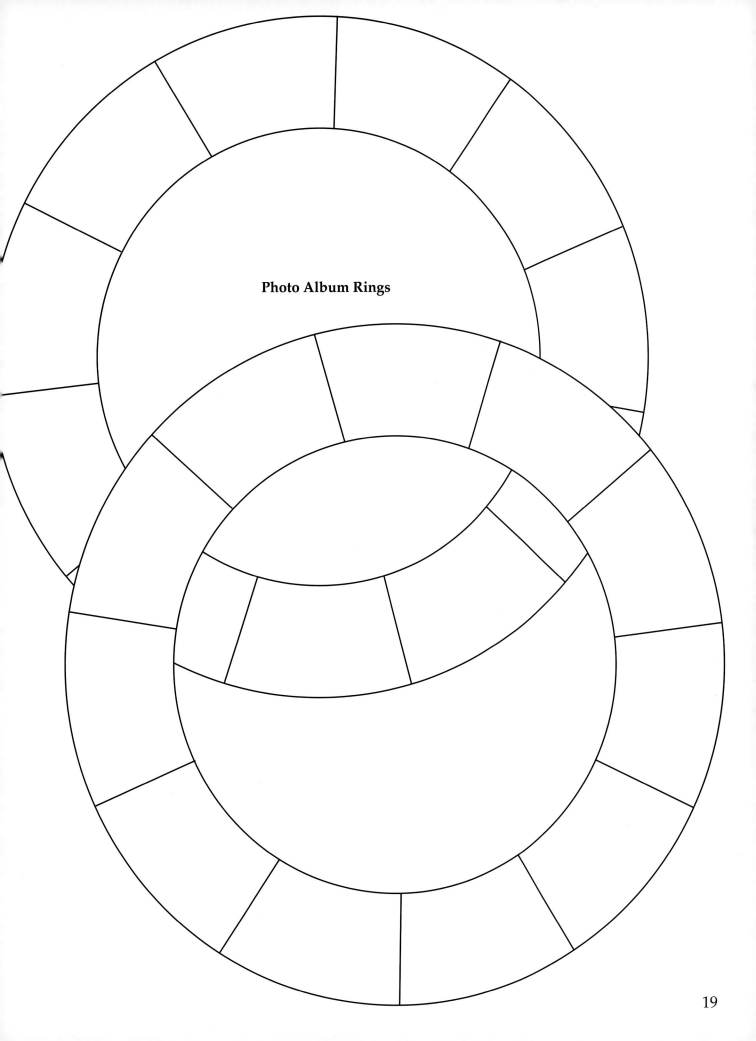

Photo Album Rings

SO-EASY STRING JACKET

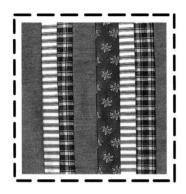

Who says cozy quilts are only for the bedroom! So easy to make, our string jacket is a fun project for using up matching scraps from your fabric stash. A plain sweatshirt provides the foundation for the fabric strips, which are added one at a time — you "quilt" them to the fleece background as you go. For a stylish finish, a placket is added to the opened front, complete with coordinating covered buttons. Whether you're going out to enjoy the brisk morning air or the blooms of early spring, this snuggly jacket will be a fitting fashion!

SO-EASY STRING JACKET

SUPPLIES

Yardage is based on 45"w fabric.

  white sweatshirt with set-in sleeves
  ³/₈ yd **each** of 4 blue print fabrics
  covered button kit
  yardstick
  seam ripper
  fabric marking pen

MAKING THE JACKET

1. Wash, dry, and press sweatshirt and fabrics.
2. Measure shirt from shoulder seam to waist ribbing; add 3". Refer to **Rotary Cutting**, page 142, to cut strips of fabric in varying widths from 1³/₄" to 2¹/₂" by the determined length measurement.
3. Lay shirt flat with front side up. Use fabric marking pen and yardstick to draw a straight line down center front of shirt and from underarm seam to waist ribbing on each side of shirt. Cut along drawn line at center shirt front only.
4. Use seam ripper to open each side of front neck ribbing ¹/₂" past each shoulder seam and each side of front waist ribbing ¹/₂" past drawn lines at sides. Open armhole seams at front of shirt ¹/₂" past shoulder seams and drawn lines at sides. Open shoulder seams.
5. Machine stitch close to raw edges of neck, front, shoulder, and bottom of shirt.
6. (*Note:* For Steps 6 - 9, use a ¹/₄" seam allowance and add strips at random.) Place 1 fabric strip right side up on shirt matching 1 long edge of strip with cut edge at center shirt front. Ends will extend beyond top and bottom edges of shirt (**Fig. 1**).

Fig. 1

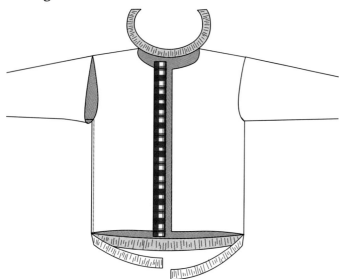

7. Lay a second strip right side down on first strip, matching 1 long edge with remaining edge of first strip; pin in place (**Fig. 2**). Stitch strip in place through all layers. Flip second strip right side up; press.

Fig. 2

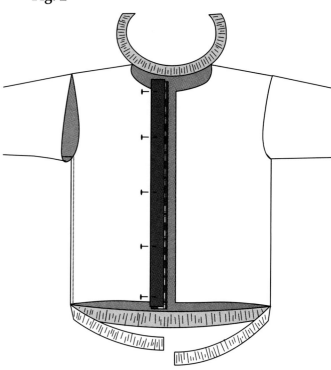

8. Continue adding strips with last strip extending at least ¹/₄" past drawn line at side of shirt. Turn edge of last strip to wrong side, matching fold along drawn line; pin in place. Stitch close to folded edge of strip.
9. Repeat Steps 6 - 8 to cover remaining front section of shirt.
10. Trim ends of strips even with top and bottom edges of shirt.
11. Stitch shirt fronts to shirt back at shoulders. Sew neck and waist ribbings to shirt fronts. Stitch armhole seams closed along previous seamlines.
12. To make placket, measure cut edge of shirt front from top to bottom; add 1". Cut 2 strips of fabric 3¹/₂" by the determined measurement.
13. Matching wrong sides, fold 1 placket piece in half lengthwise and press. Unfold placket. Press 1 long edge of placket ¹/₂" to wrong side.
14. Matching right sides, place unpressed edge of 1 placket piece on cut edge of 1 shirt front with ends extending ¹/₂" past top and bottom. Using a ¹/₂" seam allowance, stitch through all layers (**Fig. 3**). Flip placket right side up (**Fig. 4**).

Fig. 3

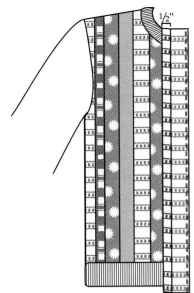

1/2"

Fig. 5

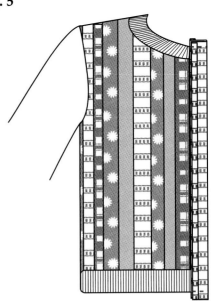

Fig. 4

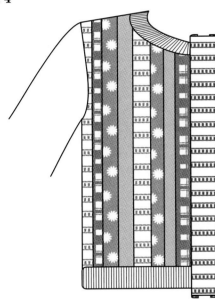

15. Matching right sides, fold placket back toward right side of shirt, matching long pressed edge of placket with placket seam. Using a 1/2" seam allowance, sew across each end of placket (**Fig. 5**). Trim seam allowance to 1/8".

16. Turn placket right side out, folding pressed edge to wrong side of shirt and covering stitching line; pin in place. Topstitch placket 1/8" from each long edge.

17. Repeat Steps 13 - 16 to attach remaining placket piece to remaining cut edge of shirt front.

18. Follow manufacturer's instructions to cover buttons with assorted fabrics.

19. Use fabric marking pen to mark placement of buttonholes on 1 placket and buttons on opposite placket. Work buttonholes and cut open. Sew on buttons.

STYLISH CAKE STAND COLLECTION

A *graceful display for baked delights, the old-fashioned cake stand has served for generations as the centerpiece for home-style celebrations. Birthdays, anniversaries, and other special get-togethers wouldn't be complete without a lovely cake presented on an elegant pedestal. Our version of the classic Cake Stand pattern is created using easy methods: the triangle-squares used to form the blocks are made with a quick grid technique. Set on point, the pieced blocks are offset with white squares and joined in diagonal rows for a stylish look. Edge the quilt with basic borders and enjoy the sweet satisfaction of simplicity!*

*P*retty flowers brighten any occasion and add a special touch to our Cake Stand wall hanging (below). The motifs are appliquéd over the pieced center block and inside the corner stars. A strip-pieced inner border adds interest, and the two-tone ribbon border produces a dimensional look. You'll be dressed in festive style wearing this embellished sweatshirt (opposite). It features a floral star block, borrowed from the wall hanging, and blanket-stitch trim. The coordinating tote is great for carrying along gifts!

STYLISH CAKE STAND QUILT

SKILL LEVEL: 1 2 **3** 4 5
BLOCK SIZE: 7¹/₂" x 7¹/₂"
QUILT SIZE: 79" x 89"

YARDAGE REQUIREMENTS
Yardage is based on 45"w fabric.

■ 4¹/₈ yds of blue solid
□ 4 yds of white solid
▨ 2¹/₂ yds of light blue solid
7¹/₄ yds for backing
1 yd for binding
90" x 108" batting

CUTTING OUT THE PIECES
All measurements include a ¹/₄" seam allowance. Follow
Rotary Cutting, page 142, to cut fabric.

1. **From blue solid:** ■
   - Cut 2 lengthwise **side outer borders**
     5¹/₂" x 93".
   - Cut 2 lengthwise **top/bottom outer borders**
     5¹/₂" x 72".
   - Cut 2 **large rectangles** 18" x 23" for large
     triangle-squares.
   - Cut 4 **rectangles** 16" x 18" for small
     triangle-squares.
   - Cut 4 strips 5"w. From these strips, cut 84
     small rectangles 2" x 5".
   - Cut 4 strips 2"w. From these strips, cut 84
     small squares 2" x 2".

2. **From white solid:** □
   - Cut 2 **large rectangles** 18" x 23" for large
     triangle-squares.
   - Cut 4 **rectangles** 16" x 18" for small
     triangle-squares.
   - Cut 6 strips 7¹/₂"w. From these strips, cut 30
     setting squares 7¹/₂" x 7¹/₂".
   - Cut 6 squares 11⁷/₈" x 11⁷/₈". Cut squares twice
     diagonally to make 24 **side triangles**. (You
     will need 22 and have 2 left over.)
   - Cut 2 squares 6¹/₄" x 6¹/₄". Cut squares once
     diagonally to make 4 **corner triangles**.

3. **From light blue solid:** ▨
   - Cut 2 lengthwise **side inner borders**
     2¹/₂" x 83".
   - Cut 2 lengthwise **top/bottom inner borders**
     2¹/₂" x 68".

ASSEMBLING THE QUILT TOP
Follow Piecing and Pressing, page 144, to make quilt top.

1. To make small triangle-squares, place 1 blue and
   1 white **rectangle** right sides together. Referring
   to **Fig. 1**, follow **Making Triangle-Squares**,
   page 145, to make 84 **small triangle-squares**.
   Repeat with remaining **rectangles** to make a
   total of 336 **small triangle-squares**.

Fig. 1

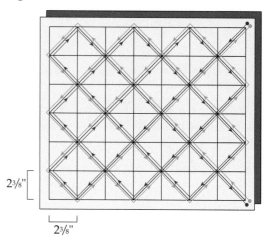

small triangle-square (make 336)

2. To make large triangle-squares, place 1 blue
   and 1 white **large rectangle** right sides together.
   Referring to **Fig. 2**, follow **Making Triangle-
   Squares**, page 145, to make 24 **large triangle-
   squares**. Repeat with remaining **large rectangles**
   to make a total of 48 **large triangle-squares**.
   (You will need 42 and have 6 left over.)

Fig. 2

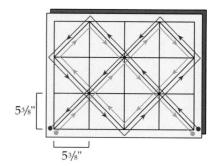

large triangle-square (make 48)

3. Sew 3 **small triangle-squares** and one **small square** together to make **Unit 1**. Make 42 **Unit 1's**.

Unit 1 (make 42)

4. Sew 3 **small triangle-squares** together to make **Unit 2**. Make 42 **Unit 2's**.

Unit 2 (make 42)

5. Sew 1 **large triangle-square**, 1 **Unit 2**, then 1 **Unit 1** together to make **Unit 3**. Make 42 **Unit 3's**.

Unit 3 (make 42)

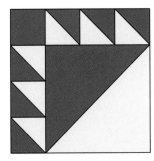

6. Sew 1 **small rectangle** and 1 **small triangle-square** together to make **Unit 4**. Make 42 **Unit 4's**.

Unit 4 (make 42)

7. Sew 1 **small square**, 1 **small triangle-square**, and 1 **small rectangle** together to make **Unit 5**. Make 42 **Unit 5's**.

Unit 5 (make 42)

8. Sew 1 **Unit 3**, 1 **Unit 4**, then 1 **Unit 5** together to make **Block**. Make 42 **Blocks**.

Block (make 42)

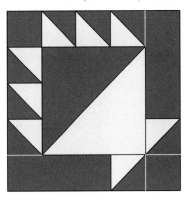

9. Referring to **Assembly Diagram**, page 30, sew **corner triangles**, **side triangles**, **setting squares**, and **Blocks** together into diagonal rows. Sew rows together to make center section of quilt top.
10. Follow **Adding Squared Borders**, page 148, to add **top**, **bottom**, then **side inner borders** to center section. Repeat to add **outer borders** to complete quilt top.

COMPLETING THE QUILT

1. Follow **Quilting**, page 149, to mark, layer, and quilt, using **Quilting Diagram** as a suggestion. Our quilt is hand quilted.
2. Cut a 32" square of binding fabric. Follow **Binding**, page 153, to bind quilt using 2$\frac{1}{2}$"w bias binding with mitered corners.

Quilting Diagram

Assembly Diagram

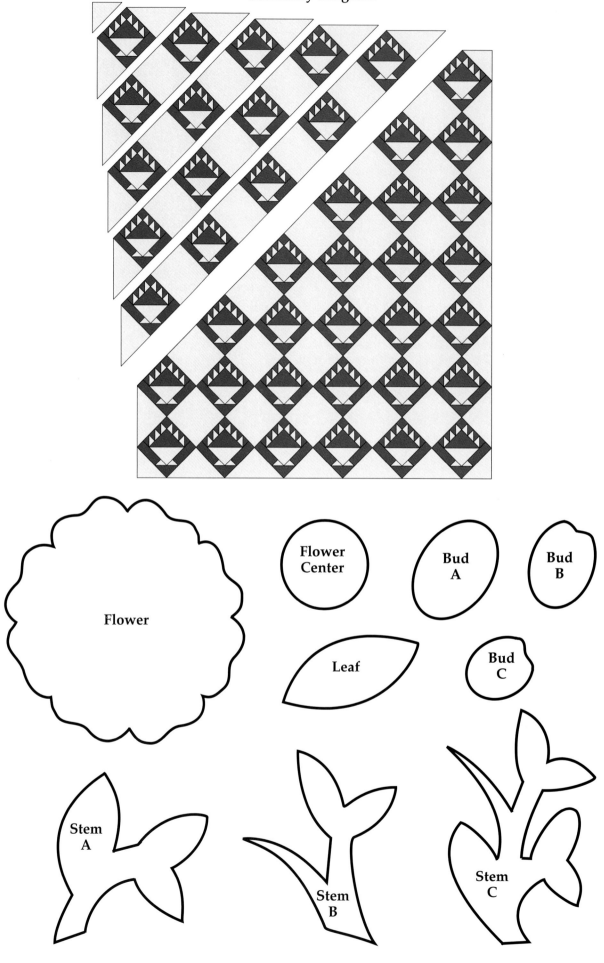

Flower

Flower Center

Bud A

Bud B

Leaf

Bud C

Stem A

Stem B

Stem C

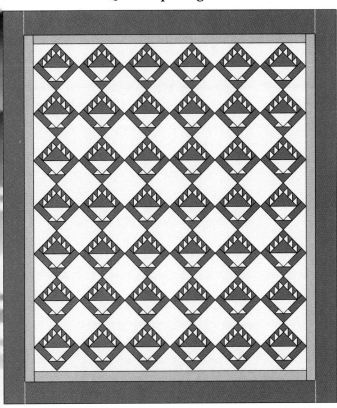

STYLISH CAKE STAND WALL HANGING

SKILL LEVEL: 1 2 3 **4** 5
WALL HANGING SIZE: 30" x 30"

YARDAGE REQUIREMENTS
Yardage is based on 45"w fabric.

⬜ ⅝ yd of white solid
⬛ ⅜ yd of blue solid
◻ ⅜ yd of light blue print
◻ ¼ yd of blue print
◼ ¼ yd of dark blue print
▨ scraps of light blue solid and blue check
  for appliqués
1 yd for backing and hanging sleeve
⅝ yd for binding
32" x 32" batting

You will also need:
  paper-backed fusible web
  transparent monofilament thread
  25 blue ¼" dia. buttons

CUTTING OUT THE PIECES
All measurements include a ¼" seam allowance. Follow
***Rotary Cutting**, page 142, to cut fabric.*

1. **From white solid:** ⬜
   - Cut 1 **square A** 6" x 6" for triangle-squares.
   - Cut 1 square 5⅜" x 5⅜". Cut square once diagonally to make 2 **triangles**. (You will need 1 and have 1 left over.)
   - Cut 4 **large rectangles** 3¾" x 8".
   - Cut 4 **square B's** 3¾" x 3¾".
   - Cut 4 squares 6⅜" x 6⅜". Cut squares once diagonally to make 8 **large triangles**.
   - Cut 7 **strips** 1½" x 7".
   - Cut 2 **square C's** 1½" x 1½".
   - Cut 4 **square D's** 3¼" x 3¼".
   - Cut 16 **small rectangles** 3¼" x 1⅞".
   - Cut 16 **small square D's** 1⅞" x 1⅞".
   - Cut 2 squares 3⅝" x 3⅝". Cut squares once diagonally to make 4 **large border triangles**.
   - Cut 8 squares 4" x 4". Cut squares twice diagonally to make 32 **small border triangles**.

2. **From blue solid:** ⬛
   - Cut 7 **strips** 1½" x 7".
   - Cut 2 **square C's** 1½" x 1½".
   - Cut 8 squares 3⅝" x 3⅝". Cut squares once diagonally to make 16 **large border triangles**.
   - Cut 4 squares 4" x 4". Cut squares twice diagonally to make 16 **small border triangles**.

3. **From light blue print:** ◻
   - Cut 32 **small square D's** 1⅞" x 1⅞".
   - Cut 10 squares 3⅝" x 3⅝". Cut squares once diagonally to make 20 **large border triangles**.
   - Cut 4 squares 4" x 4". Cut squares twice diagonally to make 16 **small border triangles**.

4. **From blue print:** ◻
   - Cut 1 **square A** 6" x 6" for triangle-squares.
   - Cut 1 square 5⅜" x 5⅜". Cut square once diagonally to make 2 **triangles**. (You will need 1 and have 1 left over.)
   - Cut 2 **small square A's** 2" x 2".
   - Cut 2 **small rectangles** 2" x 5".

5. **From dark blue print:** ◼
   - Cut 2 **top/bottom borders** 1¼" x 29½".
   - Cut 2 **side borders** 1¼" x 28".

6. **From remaining fabric and scraps:** ▨
   - Using patterns, page 30, and referring to **Wall Hanging Top Diagram**, page 34, follow **Preparing Fusible Appliqués**, page 146, to make the following appliqués:

1 **flower**	2 **leaf**
1 **flower center**	2 **bud A**
1 **stem A**	4 **bud B**
1 **stem B**	4 **bud C**
4 **stem C**	

ASSEMBLING THE WALL HANGING TOP

Follow Piecing and Pressing, page 144, to make wall hanging top.

1. To make triangle-squares, place white and blue print **square A's** right sides together. Referring to **Fig. 1**, follow **Making Triangle-Squares**, page 145, to make 8 **triangle-squares**.

Fig. 1

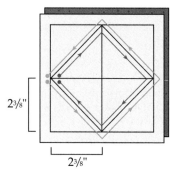

triangle-square (make 8)

2. Sew 3 **triangle-squares** together to make **Unit 1**.

Unit 1

3. Sew 3 **triangle-squares** and 1 **small square A** together to make **Unit 2**.

Unit 2

4. Sew 2 **triangles** together to make **Unit 3**.

Unit 3

5. Sew 1 **small rectangle** and 1 **triangle-square** together to make **Unit 4**.

Unit 4

6. Sew 1 **small rectangle**, 1 **triangle-square**, and 1 **small square A** together to make **Unit 5**.

Unit 5

7. Referring to **Cake Stand Block** diagram, sew **Units 1 - 5** together to make **Cake Stand Block**.

Cake Stand Block

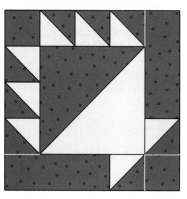

8. Sew 1 **large rectangle** each to top and bottom edges of **Cake Stand Block**. Sew 1 **square B** to each end of each remaining **large rectangle**. Sew rectangles to side edges of **Cake Stand Block** to make **Unit 6**.

Unit 6

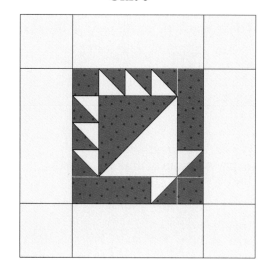

9. Sew **strips** together to make **Strip Set**. Cut across **Strip Set** at 1½" intervals to make 4 **Unit 7's**.

Strip Set   **Unit 7** (make 4)

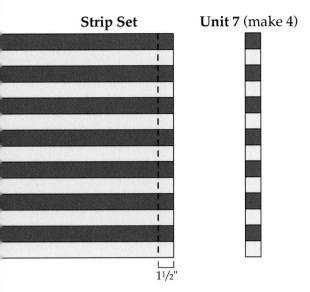

1½"

10. Sew 1 **Unit 7** each to top and bottom edges of **Unit 6**. Sew **square C's** to each end of each remaining **Unit 7**. Sew **Unit 7's** to side edges of **Unit 6** to make **Unit 8**.

Unit 8

11. Place 1 **small square D** on 1 **small rectangle** and stitch diagonally (**Fig. 2**). Trim ¼" from stitching (**Fig. 3**). Press open, pressing seam allowance toward darker fabric.

Fig. 2   **Fig. 3**

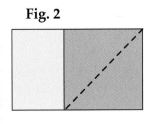

12. Place 1 **small square D** on opposite end of **small rectangle** and stitch diagonally (**Fig. 4**). Trim ¼" from stitching (**Fig. 5**). Press open, pressing seam allowance toward darker fabric, to make **Unit 9**.

Fig. 4   **Fig. 5**

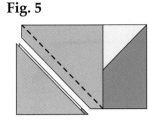

Unit 9

13. Repeat Steps 11 and 12 to make 16 **Unit 9's**.
14. Sew 1 **Unit 9** and 2 **small square D's** together to make **Unit 10**. Make 8 **Unit 10's**.

Unit 10 (make 8)

15. Sew 2 **Unit 9's** and 1 **square D** together to make **Unit 11**. Make 4 **Unit 11's**.

Unit 11 (make 4)

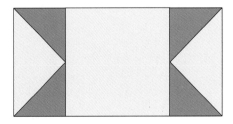

16. Sew 2 **Unit 10's** and 1 **Unit 11** together to make **Variable Star Block**. Make 4 **Variable Star Blocks**.

Variable Star Block (make 4)

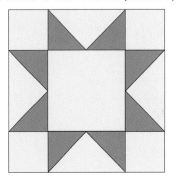

17. Sew 1 **Variable Star Block** and 2 **large triangles** together to make **Unit 12**. Make 4 **Unit 12's**.

Unit 12 (make 4)

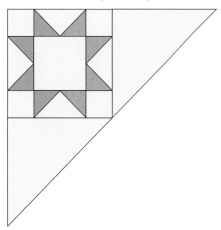

18. Referring to **Wall Hanging Top Diagram**, sew **Unit 8** and **Unit 12's** together to make center section of wall hanging top.
19. Sew 2 **large border triangles** together to make **Unit 13**. Make 4 **Unit 13's**.

Unit 13 (make 4)

20. Referring to diagrams for color placement, use **large border triangles** and **small border triangles** to make 8 *each* of **Units 14 - 17**.

Unit 14 (make 8)   **Unit 15** (make 8)

Unit 16 (make 8)   **Unit 17** (make 8)

21. Using 2 *each* of **Units 14 - 17** and referring to diagram for placement, sew units together to make **Ribbon Border Unit**. Make 4 **Ribbon Border Units**.

Ribbon Border Unit (make 4)

22. Sew 1 **Ribbon Border Unit** to each side edge of center section. Sew 1 **Unit 13** to each end of each remaining **Ribbon Border Unit**. Sew **Ribbon Border Units** to top and bottom edges of center section.
23. Sew **side**, then **top** and **bottom outer borders** to center section.
24. Referring to **Wall Hanging Top Diagram**, arrange **appliqués** on **Cake Stand Block** and **Variable Star Blocks**, overlapping as necessary; fuse in place. Follow **Invisible Appliqué**, page 146, to stitch appliqués in place to complete **Wall Hanging Top**.

COMPLETING THE WALL HANGING

1. Follow **Quilting**, page 149, to mark, layer, and quilt wall hanging, using **Quilting Diagram** as a suggestion. Our wall hanging is hand quilted.
2. Follow **Making a Hanging Sleeve**, page 155, to attach hanging sleeve to wall hanging.
3. Cut a 20" square of binding fabric. Follow **Binding**, page 153, to bind wall hanging using 2¹/₂"w bias binding with mitered corners.
4. Referring to **Wall Hanging Top Diagram**, sew buttons to front of wall hanging.

Wall Hanging Top Diagram

Quilting Diagram

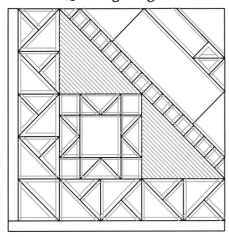

CAKE STAND SWEATSHIRT

SUPPLIES
sweatshirt
scraps of white solid, light blue print,
   blue print, and light blue solid fabrics
blue embroidery floss
paper-backed fusible web
transparent monofilament thread
6" x 6" batting
6" x 6" square of fabric for backing
5 light blue 1/4" dia. buttons
2 white 1" dia. buttons

TRIMMING THE SWEATSHIRT
*Follow **Rotary Cutting**, page 142, and **Piecing and Pressing**, page 144, to make **Variable Star Block** to trim sweatshirt.*

1. Wash, dry, and press sweatshirt and fabrics. Remove neck and waist ribbings; cut sleeves 1/4" longer than desired finished length.
2. From scraps, cut 4 white **small rectangles** 1 7/8" x 3 1/4", 4 white **small square D's** 1 7/8" x 1 7/8", 1 white **square D** 3 1/4" x 3 1/4", and 8 light blue print **small square D's** 1 7/8" x 1 7/8".
3. Using pieces cut in Step 2, refer to Steps 11 - 16 of **Assembling the Wall Hanging Top**, page 33, to make 1 **Variable Star Block** (you will need 4 **Unit 9's**, 2 **Unit 10's**, and 1 **Unit 11**).
4. Using patterns, page 30, and referring to **Wall Hanging Top Diagram**, page 34, follow **Preparing Fusible Appliqués**, page 146, to make 1 **stem C**, 1 **bud B**, and 1 **bud C** appliqué.
5. Referring to photo, arrange appliqués on block, overlapping as necessary; fuse in place. Follow **Invisible Appliqué**, page 146, to stitch appliqués in place.
6. Follow **Quilting**, page 149, to layer and quilt block in the ditch along seamlines. Sew 1/4" dia. buttons to block. Trim batting and backing 1/4" smaller than block. Press raw edges of block 1/4" to wrong side.

7. Position **Block** on front of shirt; pin or baste in place. Use 3 strands of floss to work **Blanket Stitch**, page 156, around edges of block.
8. Turn all raw edges of sweatshirt 1/4" to wrong side. Use 3 strands of floss to work **Blanket Stitch** along each folded edge.
9. For cuff on each sleeve, make a 1" pleat in sleeve (**Fig. 1**) and sew 1" dia. button over pleat.

Fig. 1

CAKE STAND TOTE BAG

SUPPLIES
a canvas tote bag large enough to accommodate
   an 11" x 11" design
scraps of white solid, blue print, dark blue print,
   blue check, and light blue solid fabrics
blue embroidery floss
paper-backed fusible web
transparent monofilament thread
5 light blue 1/4" dia. buttons

TRIMMING THE TOTE BAG
*Follow **Rotary Cutting**, page 142, and **Piecing and Pressing**, page 144, to make **Cake Stand Block** to trim tote bag.*

1. From scraps, cut 1 white **square A** 6" x 6", 1 blue print **square A** 6" x 6", 2 blue print **small square A's** 2" x 2", and 2 **small rectangles** 2" x 5". Cut 1 square 5 3/8" x 5 3/8" each from white solid and blue print; cut squares once diagonally to make **triangles**. (You will need 1 triangle of each fabric and have 1 left over.)
2. Using pieces cut in Step 1, follow Steps 1 - 7 of **Assembling the Wall Hanging Top**, page 32, to make 1 **Cake Stand Block**.
3. Using patterns, page 30, and referring to **Wall Hanging Top Diagram**, page 34, follow **Preparing Fusible Appliqués**, page 146, to make 1 **flower**, 1 **flower center**, 2 **leaves**, 1 **stem A**, 1 **stem B**, and 2 **bud A** appliqués.
4. Referring to photo, arrange appliqués on block, overlapping as necessary; fuse in place. Follow **Invisible Appliqué**, page 146, to stitch appliqués in place.
5. Press raw edges of **Block** 1/4" to wrong side. Position block on front of tote bag and pin or baste in place. Blindstitch block to tote bag.
6. Use 3 strands of floss to work **Blanket Stitch**, page 156, around top edge of tote bag.

LOST SHIPS

For the families of nineteenth-century seafarers, billowy sails disappearing over a watery horizon left only anxious hearts until the journey's end. To pass the time until her sailor's return, a quilter might have pieced the Lost Ships pattern, hoping that the patchwork vessels might somehow lead her love home again. Our variation of the ageless design, also known as Lady of the Lake, is updated with timesaving methods. We utilized a quick grid-piecing technique to produce dozens of accurate triangle-squares at a time. The blocks are then alternated with plain squares so that the motifs seem to float on a light background. A simple "harbor" is created by adding basic borders.

LOST SHIPS QUILT

SKILL LEVEL: 1 2 3 4 5
BLOCK SIZE: 7½" x 7½"
QUILT SIZE: 81" x 81"

YARDAGE REQUIREMENTS
Yardage is based on 45"w fabric.

☐ 5 yds of white solid
■ 4 yds of navy print
7½ yds for backing
1 yd for binding
90" x 108" batting

CUTTING OUT THE PIECES
All measurements include a ¼" seam allowance. Follow **Rotary Cutting***, page 142, to cut fabric.*

1. **From white solid:** ☐
   - Cut 8 strips 8"w. From these strips, cut 40 **setting squares** 8" x 8".
   - Cut 4 strips 2"w. From these strips, cut 82 **small squares** 2" x 2".
   - Cut 4 lengthwise **outer borders** 4" x 84".
   - Cut 6 **rectangles** 16" x 21" for triangle-squares.

2. **From navy print:** ■
   - Cut 6 strips 5"w. From these strips, cut 41 **squares** 5" x 5".
   - Cut 4 lengthwise **inner borders** 3" x 84".
   - Cut 6 **rectangles** 16" x 21" for triangle-squares.

ASSEMBLING THE QUILT TOP
Follow **Piecing and Pressing***, page 144, to make quilt top.*

1. To make triangle-squares, place 1 white and 1 navy **rectangle** right sides together. Referring to **Fig. 1**, follow **Making Triangle-Squares**, page 145, to make 96 **triangle-squares**. Repeat with remaining **rectangles** to make a total of 576 **triangle-squares**. (You will need 574 and have 2 left over.)

Fig. 1

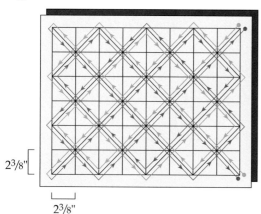

2⅜"
2⅜"

triangle-square (make 576)

2. Sew 4 **triangle-squares** and 1 **small square** together to make **Unit 1**. Make 82 **Unit 1's**.

Unit 1 (make 82)

3. Sew 3 **triangle-squares** together to make **Unit 2**. Make 82 **Unit 2's**.

Unit 2 (make 82)

4. Sew 2 **Unit 2's** and 1 **square** together to make **Unit 3**. Make 41 **Unit 3's**.

Unit 3 (make 41)

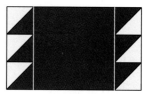

5. Sew 2 **Unit 1's** and 1 **Unit 3** together to make **Block**. Make 41 **Blocks**.

Block (make 41)

6. Sew 5 **Blocks** and 4 **setting squares** together to make **Row A**. Make 5 **Row A's**.

Row A (make 5)

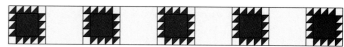

7. Sew 5 **setting squares** and 4 **Blocks** together to make **Row B**. Make 4 **Row B's**.

Row B (make 4)

8. Referring to **Quilt Top Diagram**, sew **Row A's** and **Row B's** together to make center section of quilt top.
9. Sew 1 **inner border** and 1 **outer border** together to make **Border Unit**. Make 4 **Border Units**.

Border Unit (make 4)

10. Follow **Adding Mitered Borders**, page 148, to sew **Border Units** to center section to complete **Quilt Top**.

COMPLETING THE QUILT

1. Follow **Quilting**, page 149, to mark, layer, and quilt, using **Quilting Diagram** as a suggestion. Our quilt is hand quilted.
2. Cut a 31" square of binding fabric. Follow **Binding**, page 153, to bind quilt using 2½"w bias binding with mitered corners.

Quilting Diagram

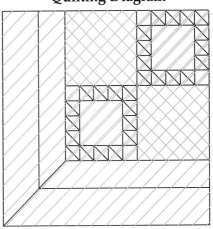

Quilt Top Diagram

HIDDEN STARS COLLECTION

Spotting the intriguing designs that can develop from the most basic quilt block is one of the essential joys of quilting. Elements such as sashing and setting squares are often used to complement a pattern, but simply placing the blocks side-by-side can create dramatic graphic interest. The squares can seem to blend together, forming new — and sometimes unexpected — designs. In our Hidden Stars quilt, for instance, the Ohio Stars you see are actually formed by small Square-in-a-Square blocks. The simple blocks are created using plain squares and triangles with alternating background colors, then joined in rows and finished with a crisp white border. For contrast, blue thread is used to complete the quilting.

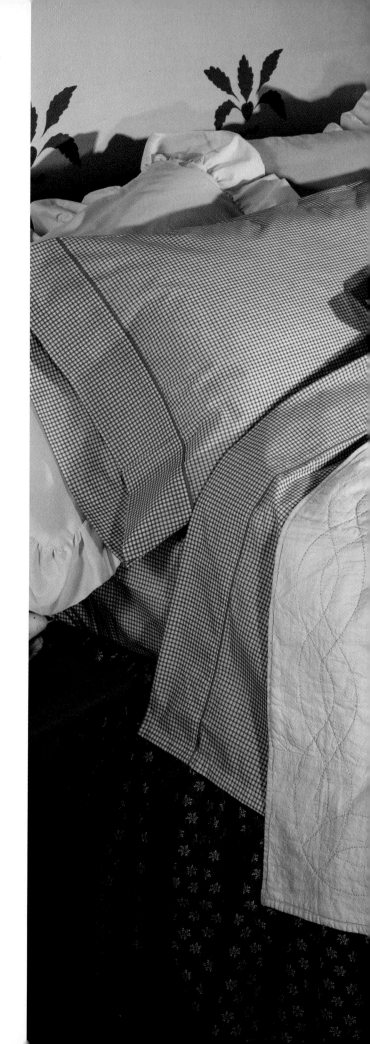

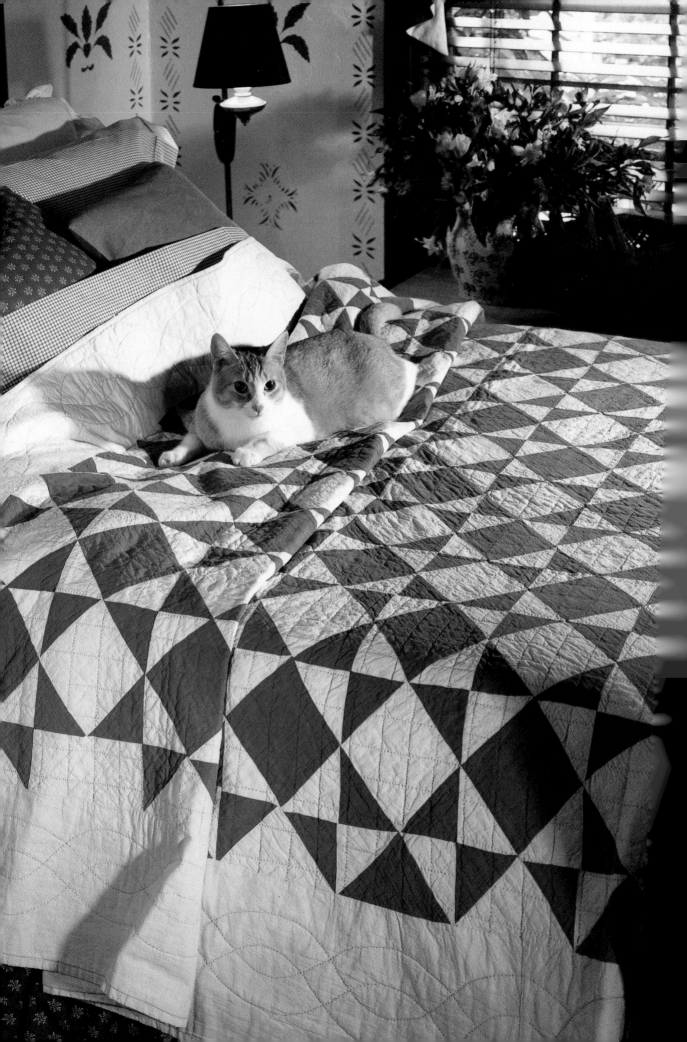

Our Hidden Stars quilt inspired stellar coordinates like this charming wall hanging (opposite). It features a Churn Dash medallion bordered by two rounds of Square-in-a-Square motifs. Enhanced with welting, the blocks are also used to neatly trim a plain sheet set (below).

HIDDEN STARS QUILT

SKILL LEVEL: 1 2 3 4 5
BLOCK SIZE: 6" x 6"
QUILT SIZE: 75" x 87"

YARDAGE REQUIREMENTS
Yardage is based on 45"w fabric.

5¼ yds of white solid
2¾ yds of blue solid
5¼ yds for backing
1 yd for binding
81" x 96" batting

CUTTING OUT THE PIECES
*All measurements include a ¼" seam allowance. Follow
Rotary Cutting, page 142, to cut fabric.*

1. **From white solid:** ☐
   - Cut 8 strips 4¾"w. From these strips, cut 60
     squares 4¾" x 4¾".
   - Cut 12 strips 3⅞"w. From these strips, cut 120
     squares 3⅞" x 3⅞". Cut squares once
     diagonally to make 240 **triangles**.
   - Cut 2 lengthwise **top/bottom borders** 7½" x 64".
   - Cut 2 lengthwise **side borders** 7½" x 90".

2. **From blue solid:** ■
   - Cut 8 strips 4¾"w. From these strips, cut 60
     squares 4¾" x 4¾".
   - Cut 12 strips 3⅞"w. From these strips, cut 120
     squares 3⅞" x 3⅞". Cut squares once
     diagonally to make 240 **triangles**.

ASSEMBLING THE QUILT TOP
Follow Piecing and Pressing, page 144, to make quilt top.

1. Sew 1 **square** and 4 **triangles** together to make
   Block A. Make 60 **Block A's**.

Block A (make 60)

2. Sew 1 **square** and 4 **triangles** together to make
   Block B. Make 60 **Block B's**.

Block B (make 60)

3. Sew 5 **Block A's** and 5 **Block B's** together to
   make **Row**. Make 12 **Rows**.

Row (make 12)

4. Referring to **Quilt Top Diagram**, sew **Rows**
   together to make center section of quilt top.
5. Follow **Adding Squared Borders**, page 148, to
   add **top**, **bottom**, then **side borders** to complete
   Quilt Top.

COMPLETING THE QUILT
1. Follow **Quilting**, page 149, to mark, layer, and
   quilt, using **Quilting Diagram** as a suggestion.
   Our quilt is hand quilted.
2. Cut a 32" square of binding fabric. Follow
   Binding, page 153, to bind quilt using 2½"w bias
   binding with mitered corners.

Quilting Diagram

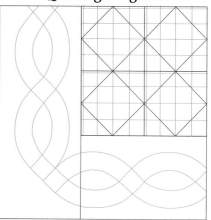

Quilt Top Diagram

HIDDEN STARS WALL HANGING

SKILL LEVEL: 1 2 3 4 5
BLOCK SIZE: 3" x 3"
WALL HANGING SIZE: 28" x 28"

YARDAGE REQUIREMENTS

Yardage is based on 45"w fabric.

☐ ³/₄ yd of white solid

■ ³/₄ yd of blue print

■ ³/₈ yd of blue plaid
  1 yd for backing and hanging sleeve
  ³/₄ yd for binding
  29" x 29" batting

CUTTING OUT THE PIECES

All measurements include a ¹/₄" seam allowance. Follow Rotary Cutting, page 142, to cut fabric.

1. **From white solid:** ☐
   - Cut 2 strips 2⁵/₈"w. From these strips, cut 24 **squares** 2⁵/₈" x 2⁵/₈".
   - Cut 3 strips 2³/₈"w. From these strips, cut 48 squares 2³/₈" x 2³/₈". Cut squares once diagonally to make 96 **triangles**.
   - Cut 1 **rectangle** 6¹/₂" x 12" for triangle-squares.
   - Cut 5 **large squares** 2³/₄" x 2³/₄".

2. **From blue print:** ■
   - Cut 2 strips 2⁵/₈"w. From these strips, cut 24 **squares** 2⁵/₈" x 2⁵/₈".
   - Cut 3 strips 2³/₈"w. From these strips, cut 48 squares 2³/₈" x 2³/₈". Cut squares once diagonally to make 96 **triangles**.
   - Cut 1 **rectangle** 6¹/₂" x 12" for triangle-squares.
   - Cut 4 **large squares** 2³/₄" x 2³/₄".

3. **From blue plaid:** ■
   - Cut 4 strips ⁷/₈" x 14" for **narrow borders**.
   - Cut 4 strips 2" x 29" for **outer borders**.

ASSEMBLING THE WALL HANGING TOP

Follow Piecing and Pressing, page 144, to make wall hanging top.

1. To make triangle-squares, place blue and white **rectangles** right sides together. Referring to **Fig. 1**, follow **Making Triangle-Squares**, page 145, to make 4 **triangle-squares**.

Fig. 1

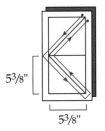

5³/₈"

5³/₈"

triangle-square (make 4)

2. Sew 2 **large squares** together to make **Unit 1**. Make 4 **Unit 1's**.

Unit 1 (make 4)

3. Sew **triangle-squares**, **Unit 1's**, and **large square** together to make 1 **Churn Dash Block**.

Churn Dash Block (make 1)

4. Follow **Adding Squared Borders**, page 148, to add **top**, **bottom**, then **side narrow borders** to **Churn Dash Block**.

5. Follow Steps 1 and 2 of **Assembling the Quilt Top**, page 44, to make 24 **Block A's** and 24 **Block B's**.

6. Sew 4 **Block A's** and 4 **Block B's** together to make **Unit 2**. Make 4 **Unit 2's**.

Unit 2 (make 4)

7. Sew 4 **Block B's** and 4 **Block A's** together to make **Unit 3**. Make 2 **Unit 3's**.

Unit 3 (make 2)

8. Referring to **Assembly Diagram**, page 46, sew **Unit 2's**, **Unit 3's**, and **Churn Dash Block** together to make center section of wall hanging top.

9. Follow **Adding Squared Borders**, page 148, to add **top**, **bottom**, then **side outer borders** to complete **Wall Hanging Top**.

45

COMPLETING THE WALL HANGING

1. Follow **Quilting**, page 149, to mark, layer, and quilt wall hanging, using **Quilting Diagram** as a suggestion. Our wall hanging is hand quilted.
2. Follow **Making a Hanging Sleeve**, page 155, to attach hanging sleeve to wall hanging.
3. Cut a 20" square of binding fabric. Follow **Binding**, page 153, to bind wall hanging using 2¹/₂"w bias binding with mitered corners.

Quilting Diagram

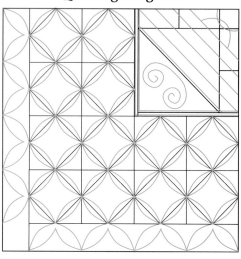

Assembly Diagram

46

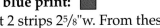

Wall Hanging Top Diagram

TRIMMED SHEET AND PILLOWCASES

YARDAGE

Yardage is based on 45"w fabric.

☐ ¹/₂ yd of white solid

◼ ¹/₂ yd of blue print

◼ ³/₄ yd of blue plaid

7 yds of ¹/₈" cord for welting

You will also need:

1 double sized flat sheet (81" x 102")

2 standard pillowcases (20" x 26")

CUTTING OUT THE PIECES

All measurements include a ¹/₄" seam allowance. Follow Rotary Cutting, page 142, to cut fabric.

1. **From white solid:** ☐
   - Cut 2 strips 2⁵/₈"w. From these strips, cut 20 **squares** 2⁵/₈" x 2⁵/₈".
   - Cut 3 strips 2³/₈"w. From these strips, cut 38 squares 2³/₈" x 2³/₈". Cut squares once diagonally to make 76 **triangles**.

2. **From blue print:** ◼
   - Cut 2 strips 2⁵/₈"w. From these strips, cut 19 **squares** 2⁵/₈" x 2⁵/₈".
   - Cut 3 strips 2³/₈"w. From these strips, cut 40 squares 2³/₈" x 2³/₈". Cut squares once diagonally to make 80 **triangles**.

3. **From blue plaid:** ◼
   - Cut 1 **large square** 20" x 20".
   - Cut 4 **rectangles** 1¹/₂" x 3¹/₂".

TRIMMING THE SHEET AND PILLOWCASES

1. Wash, dry, and press sheet and pillowcases.
2. Follow Steps 1 and 2 of **Assembling the Quilt Top**, page 44, to make 20 **Block A's** and 19 **Block B's**.
3. Referring to photo, sew 14 **Block A's** and 13 **Block B's** together to make **Sheet Trim**.
4. Sew 3 **Block A's**, 3 **Block B's**, and 2 **rectangles** together to make **Pillowcase Trim**. Make 2 **Pillowcase Trims**.

Pillowcase Trim (make 2)

5. Use **large square** and follow Steps 1 - 7 of **Making Continuous Bias Strip Binding**, page 153, to make approximately 7 yds of 1¹/₂"w bias strip.
6. Follow Step 2 of **Adding Welting to Pillow Top**, page 155, to make welting, trimming seam allowance to ¹/₄".
7. Matching right sides and raw edges, stitch welting to each long edge of **Sheet Trim** and **Pillowcase Trims**. Press seam allowances toward trims. Press raw ends of trim under ¹/₄" and baste in place.
8. Referring to photo, position trims on sheet and pillowcases and pin or baste in place. Stitch through all layers in the ditch between trim and welting. Remove basting threads.

BUILDING BLOCKS

For stitchers in the 1800's, quilting was not merely a household task; it was often their only canvas for artistic expression. Many delighted in exploring the subtleties of color and shadow and became especially fond of designs that created the illusion of depth. One of those favorites was the Building Blocks pattern, also known as Tumbling Blocks or Baby Blocks. For our version, we used three shades of blue to accentuate the design's dimensional effect. The diamond pieces are easy to make without templates — simply align the fabric strips with the angle guides on your rotary cutting ruler and trim! The diamond and triangle motifs are then assembled in units to avoid awkward set-in seams.

BUILDING BLOCKS QUILT

SKILL LEVEL: 1 2 3 4 5
QUILT SIZE: 96" x 112"

YARDAGE REQUIREMENTS
Yardage is based on 45"w fabric.

- 6$\frac{1}{8}$ yds of dark blue print
- 4$\frac{7}{8}$ yds of blue print
- 3$\frac{3}{8}$ yds of light blue print
  8$\frac{3}{4}$ yds for backing
  1 yd for binding
  120" x 120" batting

CUTTING OUT THE PIECES
All measurements include a $\frac{1}{4}$" seam allowance. Follow Rotary Cutting, page 142, to cut fabric.

1. **From dark blue print:** ■
   - Cut 22 **narrow strips** 3"w.
   - Cut 12 **wide strips** 3$\frac{1}{4}$"w.
   - Cut 4 lengthwise **outer borders** 8" x 100".

2. **From blue print:** ■
   - Cut 22 **narrow strips** 3"w.
   - Cut 2 lengthwise **side inner borders** 3" x 95".
   - Cut 2 lengthwise **top/bottom inner borders** 3" x 85".
   - From remaining fabric width, cut 19 crosswise **wide strips** 3$\frac{1}{4}$"w.

3. **From light blue print:** ■
   - Cut 22 **narrow strips** 3"w.
   - Cut 12 **wide strips** 3$\frac{1}{4}$"w.

ASSEMBLING THE QUILT TOP
Follow Piecing and Pressing, page 144, to make quilt top.

1. Referring to **Fig. 1**, align 60° marking on ruler (shown in pink) with lower edge of 1 dark blue **narrow strip**. Cut along right side of ruler to cut 1 end of strip at a 60° angle.

Fig. 1

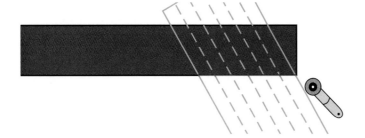

2. Turn cut **strip** 180° on mat and align 60° marking on ruler with lower edge of strip. Align previously cut 60° edge with 3" marking on ruler. Cut strip at 3" intervals as shown in **Fig. 2** to cut diamonds.

Fig. 2

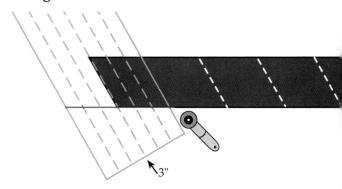

3. Repeat Steps 1 and 2 using remaining dark blue, blue, and light blue **narrow strips** to cut a total of 220 **dark blue diamonds**, 220 **blue diamonds**, and 220 **light blue diamonds**.

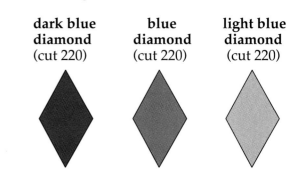

| dark blue diamond (cut 220) | blue diamond (cut 220) | light blue diamond (cut 220) |

4. Cutting diamonds at 3$\frac{1}{4}$" intervals, repeat Steps 1 and 2 using dark blue, blue, and light blue **wide strips** to cut a total of 110 **dark blue diamonds**, 110 **blue diamonds**, and 110 **light blue diamonds**. Referring to **Fig. 3**, cut across diamonds to make a total of 220 **dark blue triangles**, 220 **blue triangles**, and 220 **light blue triangles**.

Fig. 3

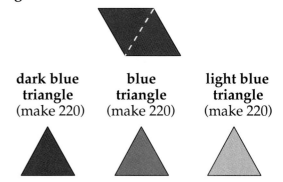

dark blue triangle (make 220)   blue triangle (make 220)   light blue triangle (make 220)

5. Sew 1 **blue diamond**, 1 **dark blue diamond**, and 1 **light blue triangle** together to make **Unit 1**. Make 220 **Unit 1's**.

Unit 1 (make 220)

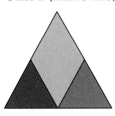

6. Sew 1 **light blue diamond**, 1 **dark blue triangle**, and 1 **blue triangle** together to make **Unit 2**. Make 220 **Unit 2's**.

Unit 2 (make 220)

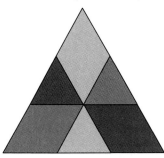

7. Sew 1 **Unit 1** and 1 **Unit 2** together to make **Unit 3**. Make 220 **Unit 3's**.

Unit 3 (make 220)

8. Referring to **Assembly Diagram**, page 52, sew 22 **Unit 3's** together to make 1 vertical row. Make 10 vertical rows; sew rows together.

9. To trim top and bottom edges straight, refer to **Fig. 4** to line up ¼" marking on ruler (shown in pink) with seam intersections. Trim off excess to make center section of quilt top.

Fig. 4

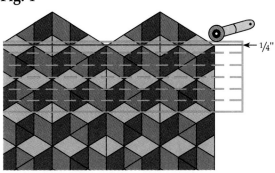

10. Follow **Adding Squared Borders**, page 148, to sew **side**, then **top** and **bottom inner borders** to center section. Repeat to add **outer borders** to complete **Quilt Top**.

COMPLETING THE QUILT

1. Follow **Quilting**, page 149, to mark, layer, and quilt, using **Quilting Diagram** as a suggestion. Our quilt is hand quilted.

2. Cut a 34" square of binding fabric. Follow **Binding**, page 153, to bind quilt using 2½"w bias binding with overlapped corners.

Quilting Diagram

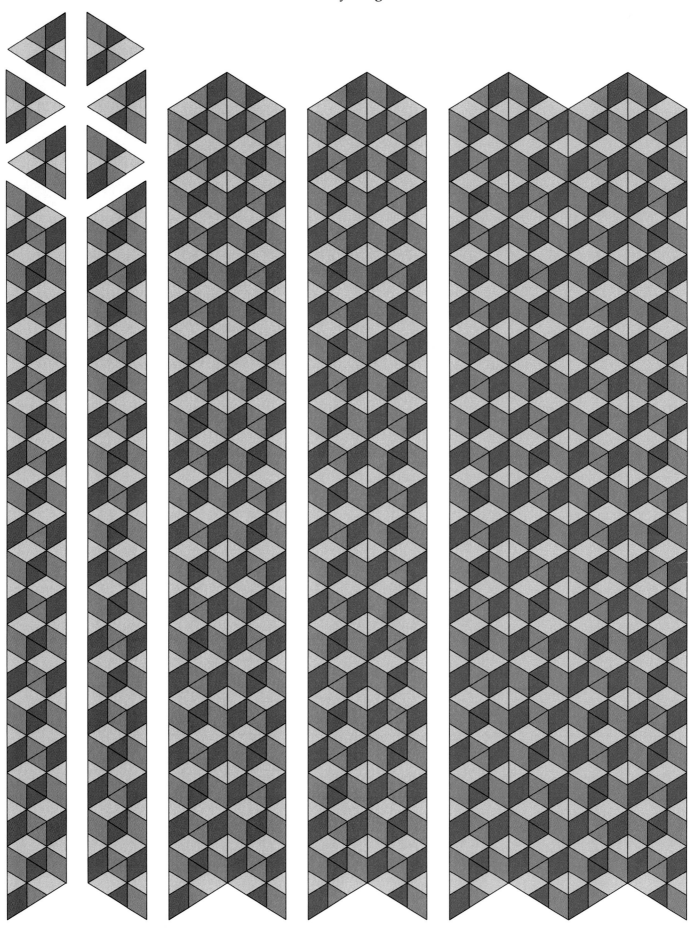

HEART-WARMING WALL HANGINGS

Quilted wall hangings came into vogue amid the nostalgia of America's Bicentennial Celebration. No longer viewed as a task of necessity, quilting appealed to a new generation that recognized the creative possibilities of the craft. In addition to traditional quilts, stitchers enjoyed making smaller ornamental pieces that were more versatile for home decorating. Our collection of charming wall hangings reflects the appeal of old-fashioned folk art. The sweet wall hanging shown here features bird, heart, and leaf motifs that are simple to machine appliqué. The homey look is enhanced with easy patchwork strips, prairie point trim, and button accents.

*P*atchwork and appliqué techniques combine to create this pleasing wall hanging (opposite). The basic pieced blocks are made with easy methods such as grid-piecing and strip sets. Decorative quilting adds a fun touch to the machine-appliquéd motifs. Our unique wreath (below) brings to mind the comforts of heart and home. Cut from Courthouse Steps blocks, the hearts are stuffed and then stitched together.

BIRD WALL HANGING

SKILL LEVEL: 1 2 *3* 4 5
WALL HANGING SIZE: 20" x 29"

YARDAGE REQUIREMENTS

Yardage is based on 45"w fabric.

▢ ¹/₄ yd of cream solid

▨ ¹/₄ yd of light blue print

■ ¹/₄ yd of dark blue print

◪ ¹/₄ yd total of assorted blue, cream, and tan prints
1 yd for backing and hanging sleeve
¹/₄ yd for binding
22" x 31" batting

You will also need:
paper-backed fusible web
transparent monofilament thread
assorted buttons

CUTTING OUT THE PIECES

All measurements include a ¹/₄" seam allowance. Follow
***Rotary Cutting**, page 142, to cut fabric.*

1. **From cream solid:** ▢
   • Cut 1 **C** 7¹/₄" x 14¹/₄".
   • Cut 1 **D** 3¹/₄" x 14¹/₄".

2. **From light blue print:** ▨
   • Cut 2 **E's** 6¹/₂" x 17".
   • Cut 2 **A's** 2¹/₂" x 14¹/₄".

3. **From dark blue print:** ■
   • Cut 2 **top/bottom borders** 1¹/₂" x 26¹/₄".
   • Cut 2 **side borders** 1¹/₂" x 19".
   • Cut 1 **B** 1" x 14¹/₄".
   • Cut 10 **squares** 3" x 3" for prairie points.

4. **From assorted blue, cream, and tan prints:** ◪
   • Cut 22 **small squares** 1³/₄" x 1³/₄".
   • Referring to photo, use patterns, pages 63 and
     64, and follow **Preparing Fusible Appliqués**,
     page 146, to make the following appliqués:
     1 **bird**   1 **large branch**
     1 **wing**   4 **small branches** (2 in reverse)
     2 **bird legs**   18 **leaves** (8 in reverse)
     6 **small hearts**

ASSEMBLING THE WALL HANGING TOP

*Follow **Piecing and Pressing**, page 144, to make wall
hanging top.*

1. Sew 11 **small squares** together to make **Unit 1**.
   Make 2 **Unit 1's**.

Unit 1 (make 2)

2. Sew **A's**, **B**, **C**, **Unit 1's**, and **D** together to make
   Unit 2.

Unit 2

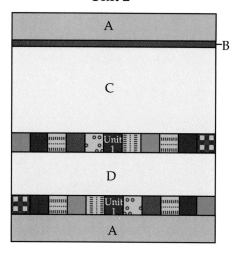

3. To make prairie points, fold each **square** in half
   with wrong sides together. Make 2 more
   diagonal folds, as shown in **Fig. 1**; press.

Fig. 1

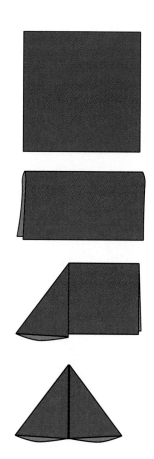

4. Referring to **Fig. 2**, baste prairie points to sides of
   Unit 2. Sew **Unit 2** and **E's** together, enclosing
   raw edges of prairie points in seam. Open and
   press to make center section of wall hanging.

Fig. 2

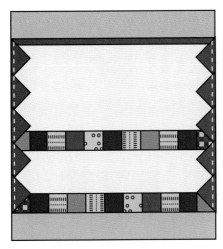

5. Sew **top**, **bottom**, then **side borders** to center section.

6. Referring to **Wall Hanging Top Diagram**, arrange appliqués on wall hanging top, overlapping as necessary. Following **Invisible Appliqué**, page 146, stitch appliqués in place to complete **Wall Hanging Top**.

COMPLETING THE WALL HANGING

1. Follow **Quilting**, page 149, to mark, layer, and quilt wall hanging, using **Quilting Diagram** as a suggestion. Our wall hanging is hand quilted.

2. Follow **Making a Hanging Sleeve**, page 155, to attach hanging sleeve to wall hanging.

3. Follow **Binding**, page 153, to bind wall hanging using 2¹/₂"w straight-grain binding with mitered corners.

4. Referring to photo, sew buttons to front of wall hanging.

Wall Hanging Top Diagram

Quilting Diagram

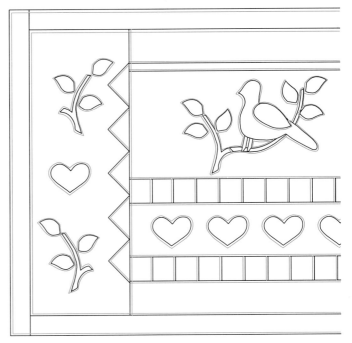

BIRDHOUSES WALL HANGING

SKILL LEVEL: 1 2 3 4 5
BLOCK SIZE: 6" x 6"
WALL HANGING SIZE: 25" x 29"

YARDAGE REQUIREMENTS
Yardage is based on 45"w fabric.

- ³/₈ yd of cream stripe
- ³/₈ yd of blue print
- ³/₈ yd of tan stripe
- ¹/₄ yd of blue stripe
- ¹/₈ yd of blue check
- ¹/₄ yd **total** of assorted blue prints and plaids
- ¹/₄ yd **total** of assorted cream prints and plaids
  1 yd for backing and hanging sleeve
  ⁵/₈ yd for binding
  26" x 30" batting

You will also need:
  paper-backed fusible web
  transparent monofilament thread

CUTTING OUT THE PIECES
All measurements include a ¹/₄" seam allowance. Follow Rotary Cutting, page 142, to cut fabric.

1. **From cream stripe:**
   • Cut 1 **background** 9" x 13".

2. **From blue print:**
   • Cut 1 **square** 11" x 11" for triangle-squares.
   • Cut 16 **small squares** 2" x 2".

3. **From tan stripe:**
   - Cut 1 **square** 11" x 11" for triangle-squares.
4. **From blue stripe:**
   - Cut 2 **side borders** 3¹/₂" x 22¹/₂".
   - Cut 2 **top/bottom borders** 3¹/₂" x 18¹/₂".
   - Cut 2 **top/bottom inner borders** 1¹/₄" x 13".
   - Cut 2 **side inner borders** 1¹/₄" x 10¹/₂".
5. **From blue check:**
   - Cut 8 **large squares** 3¹/₂" x 3¹/₂".
6. **From assorted blue prints and plaids:**
   - Cut 12 **medium squares** 2¹/₂" x 2¹/₂".
7. **From assorted cream prints and plaids:**
   - Cut 16 **medium squares** 2¹/₂" x 2¹/₂".
8. **From remaining fabrics and scraps:**
   - Referring to photo, use patterns, page 65, and follow **Preparing Fusible Appliqués**, page 146, to make the following appliqués:

2 **birdhouse A**	1 **birdhouse B**
2 **roof A**	1 **roof B**
2 **door A**	2 **door B**
1 *each* of **post A**, **post B**, and **post C**	

ASSEMBLING THE WALL HANGING TOP

*Follow **Piecing and Pressing**, page 144, to make wall hanging top.*

1. To make triangle-squares, place blue print and tan stripe **squares** right sides together. Referring to **Fig. 1**, follow **Making Triangle-Squares**, page 145, to make 32 **triangle-squares**.

Fig. 1

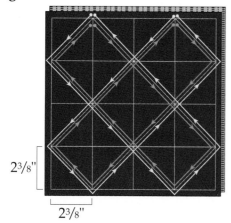

2³/₈"

2³/₈"

triangle-square (make 32)

2. Sew 2 **triangle-squares** together to make **Unit 1**. Make 16 **Unit 1's**.

Unit 1 (make 16)

3. Sew 2 **small squares** and 1 **Unit 1** together to make **Unit 2**. Make 8 **Unit 2's**.

Unit 2 (make 8)

4. Sew 2 **Unit 1's** and 1 **large square** together to make **Unit 3**. Make 4 **Unit 3's**.

Unit 3 (make 4)

5. Sew 2 **Unit 2's** and 1 **Unit 3** together to make **Star Block**. Make 4 **Star Blocks**.

Star Block (make 4)

6. Sew 9 **medium squares** together to make **Nine Patch Block**. Make 2 **Nine Patch Blocks**.

Nine Patch Block (make 2)

7. Sew 5 **medium squares** together to make **Unit 4**. Make 2 **Unit 4's**.

Unit 4 (make 2)

8. Referring to **Wall Hanging Top Diagram**, arrange **appliqués** on **background**, overlapping as necessary, and fuse in place. Follow **Invisible Appliqué**, page 146, to stitch around appliqués.

9. Sew **top, bottom**, then **side inner borders** to **background**. Sew 1 **Unit 4** to each side edge of **background** to make **Row A**.

Row A

10. Sew 2 **Star Blocks** and 1 **Nine Patch Block** together to make **Row B**. Make 2 **Row B's**.

Row B (make 2)

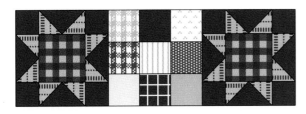

11. Referring to **Wall Hanging Top Diagram**, sew **Rows** together to make center section of wall hanging top.
12. Sew 1 **side border** to each side edge of center section. Sew 1 **large square** to each end of each **top/bottom border**. Sew **borders** to top and bottom edges of center section to complete **Wall Hanging Top**.

COMPLETING THE WALL HANGING
1. Follow **Quilting**, page 149, to mark, layer, and quilt wall hanging, using **Quilting Diagram** as a suggestion. Our wall hanging is hand quilted.
2. Follow **Making a Hanging Sleeve**, page 155, to attach hanging sleeve to wall hanging.
3. Cut a 19" square of binding fabric. Follow **Binding**, page 153, to bind wall hanging using 2 1/2"w bias binding with mitered corners.

Quilting Diagram

Wall Hanging Top Diagram

HEART WREATH

WREATH SIZE: 16" dia.

SUPPLIES

 1 **strip** 2" x 14" of cream print fabric
 2 **strips** 1" x 14" of blue print fabric
 2 **strips** 1¼" x 42" *each* of 3 cream print fabrics
   and 3 blue print fabrics
 6 **rectangles** 6½" x 8" of blue print fabric
 polyester fiberfill
 12" dia. wooden embroidery hoop
 tracing paper

PIECING THE BLOCKS

*Follow **Piecing and Pressing**, page 144, to make blocks.*

1. Sew 14"l cream and blue print **strips** together to
   make **Strip Set**. Cut across **Strip Set** at 2"
   intervals to make 6 **Unit 1's**.

Strip Set

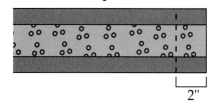

Unit 1 (make 6)

2. Place 1 cream print **strip** on 1 **Unit 1** with right
   sides together and matching 1 long raw edge of
   Unit 1. Stitch as shown in **Fig. 1**. Trim **strip** even
   with **Unit 1** (**Fig. 2**); open and press (**Fig. 3**).

Fig. 1

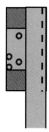

Fig. 2

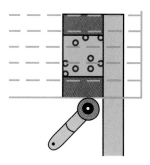

Fig. 3

3. Repeat Step 2 to add matching cream print **strip**
   to opposite edge of **Unit 1** to make **Unit 2**.

Unit 2

4. Repeat Step 2 to add 2 matching blue print **strips**
   to **Unit 2** to make **Unit 3**.

Unit 3

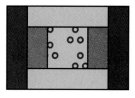

5. Continue to add **strips**, alternating 2 matching
   cream print and 2 matching blue print **strips**,
   until there are 3 **strips** on each side of **Unit 1** to
   complete **Block**.

Block

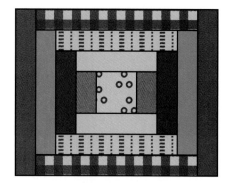

5. Repeat Steps 2 - 5 to make 6 **Blocks**.

MAKING THE WREATH

1. Use tracing paper to trace **Heart** pattern, page 64; cut out.
2. Center pattern on wrong side of 1 **rectangle**; draw around pattern. Do not cut out. Repeat with remaining **rectangles**.
3. To make stuffed hearts, place 1 **Block** and 1 **rectangle** right sides together. Leaving a 2" opening for turning, stitch directly on drawn line. Trim seam allowance to ¼".
4. Turn heart right side out and press. Stuff with fiberfill and sew opening closed by hand.
5. Using remaining **Blocks** and **rectangles**, repeat Steps 3 and 4 to make a total of 6 stuffed hearts.
6. Referring to **Fig. 4**, tack hearts together at sides to form a circle.
7. Place circle of hearts right side down on a flat surface. Center inner ring only from embroidery hoop on circle. Hand stitch stuffed hearts to hoop.

Fig. 4

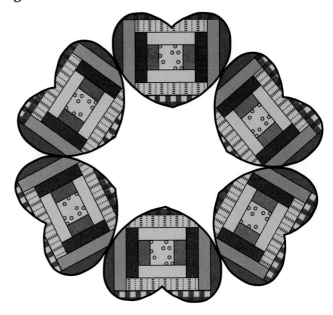

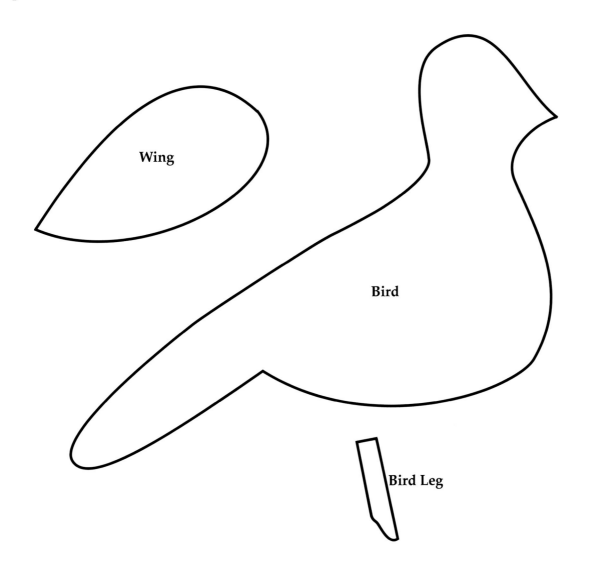

Wing

Bird

Bird Leg

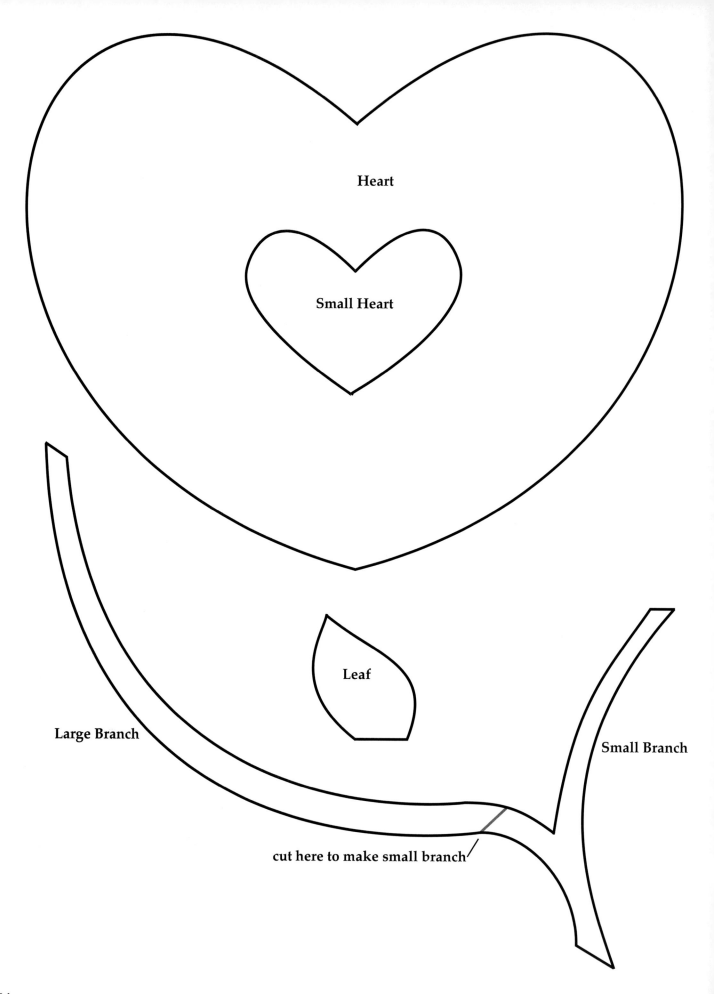

Heart

Small Heart

Leaf

Large Branch

Small Branch

cut here to make small branch

64

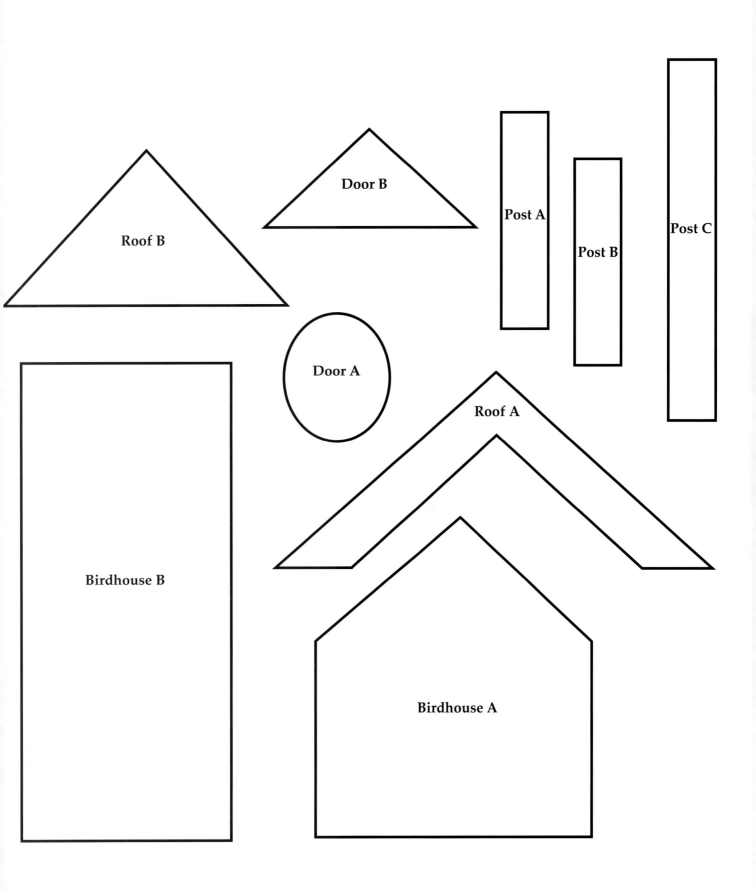

Roof B

Door B

Post A

Post B

Post C

Door A

Birdhouse B

Roof A

Birdhouse A

ENDLESS STARS

On a crisp, clear night, the midnight sky is brightened by an infinite array of twinkling stars. Those shimmering constellations no doubt inspired our Endless Stars pattern, which is traditionally known as Prairie Star. Although they appear to involve difficult angles, the stellar motifs of our quilt are quite simple to make — no templates are used at all! The angle markings on your rotary cutting ruler are the only guides you'll need to create perfect diamonds. Join them with basic triangles and large plain squares and watch the celestial show emerge!

ENDLESS STARS QUILT

SKILL LEVEL: 1 2 3 **4** 5
QUILT SIZE: 73" x 82"

YARDAGE REQUIREMENTS
Yardage is based on 45"w fabric.

☐ 4 yds of white solid
■ 2³/4 yds of blue print
5 yds for backing
1 yd for binding
81" x 96" batting

CUTTING OUT THE PIECES
All measurements include a ¹/4" seam allowance. Follow Rotary Cutting, page 142, to cut fabric.

1. **From white solid:** ☐
   - Cut 8 **strips** 4¹/2"w.
   - Cut 2 lengthwise **side outer borders** 3³/4" x 86".
   - Cut 2 lengthwise **top/bottom outer borders** 3³/4" x 77".
   - From remaining fabric width, cut 7 strips 8¹/2"w. From these strips, cut 21 **large squares** 8¹/2" x 8¹/2".
   - Cut 4 squares 12⁵/8" x 12⁵/8". Cut squares twice diagonally to make 16 **side triangles**. (You will need 13 and have 3 left over.)
   - Cut 1 square 6⁵/8" x 6⁵/8". Cut square once diagonally to make 2 **corner triangles**.

2. **From blue print:** ■
   - Cut 2 lengthwise **side inner borders** 2¹/4" x 86".
   - Cut 2 lengthwise **top/bottom inner borders** 2¹/4" x 77".
   - From remaining fabric width, cut 12 strips 5¹/4"w. Place 2 strips right sides together. From pairs of strips, cut 56 pairs of rectangles 3" x 5¹/4". Referring to **Fig. 1**, cut each pair of rectangles once diagonally to make a total of 224 (112 in reverse) **right triangles**.

Fig. 1

3"

right triangles (cut 224)

- Cut 3 strips 5¹/8"w. From these strips, cut 21 **squares** 5¹/8" x 5¹/8".
- Cut 4 squares 7⁷/8" x 7⁷/8". Cut squares twice diagonally to make 16 **small side triangles**. (You will need 13 and have 3 left over.)
- Cut 1 square 4¹/4" x 4¹/4". Cut square once diagonally to make 2 **small corner triangles**.

ASSEMBLING THE QUILT TOP
Follow Piecing and Pressing, page 144, to make quilt top.

1. Referring to **Fig. 2**, align 60° marking (shown in pink) on ruler with lower edge of 1 **strip**. Cut along right side of ruler to cut 1 end of strip at a 60° angle.

Fig. 2

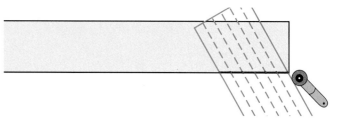

2. Turn cut **strip** 180° on mat and align 60° marking on ruler with lower edge of strip. Align previously cut 60° edge with 4¹/2" marking on ruler. Cut **strip** at 4¹/2" intervals as shown in **Fig. 3**.

Fig. 3

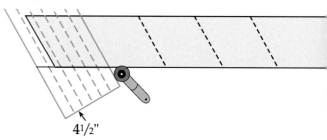

4¹/2"

3. Repeat Steps 1 and 2 with remaining **strips** to cut a total of 56 **diamonds**.

diamond (cut 56)

4. Sew 1 **diamond** and 4 **right triangles** together to make **Unit 1**. Make 56 **Unit 1's**.

Unit 1 (make 56)

5. Referring to **Assembly Diagram**, page 70, sew **corner triangles**, **small side triangles**, **Unit 1's**, **squares**, **side triangles**, **large squares**, and **small corner triangles** together into diagonal rows. Sew rows together to make center section of quilt top.

6. Sew **side inner borders** and **side outer borders** together to make **Side Border Unit**. Make 2 **Side Border Units**. Sew **top/bottom inner borders** and **top/bottom outer borders** together to make **Top/Bottom Border Unit**. Make 2 **Top/Bottom Border Units**.

Border Unit

7. Referring to **Quilt Top Diagram**, page 71, follow **Adding Mitered Borders**, page 148, to sew **Border Units** to center section to complete **Quilt Top**.

COMPLETING THE QUILT
1. Follow **Quilting**, page 149, to mark, layer, and quilt, using **Quilting Diagram** as a suggestion. Our quilt is hand quilted.
2. Cut a 30" square of binding fabric. Follow **Binding**, page 153, to bind quilt using 2$\frac{1}{2}$"w bias binding with mitered corners.

Quilting Diagram

CHURN DASH MAZE

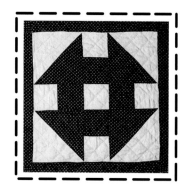

In pioneer families, even the youngest members diligently shared in the daily chores. Children took on such basic duties as gathering eggs and milking the cow. Then in the evening, while their mothers quilted, the youngsters often took turns pumping a churn dash to make rich cream and butter. Named for that rough-hewn tool, the Churn Dash design is a true quilting classic. The blocks in our version were made by strip-piecing the center sections and grid-piecing the triangle-square corners. The blocks were arranged with a sashing design known as Garden Maze that creates a neat frame for each square. Displayed as a unique accent for the kitchen table, this quilt conveys the beauty and simplicity of homemade goodness.

CHURN DASH MAZE QUILT

SKILL LEVEL: 1 2 3 4 5
BLOCK SIZE: 11¼" x 11¼"
QUILT SIZE: 74" x 90"

YARDAGE REQUIREMENTS
Yardage is based on 45"w fabric.

- ☐ 4¾ yds of cream solid
- ■ 4½ yds of navy print
- 5½ yds for backing
- 1 yd for binding
- 81" x 96" batting

CUTTING OUT THE PIECES
*All measurements include a ¼" seam allowance. Follow **Rotary Cutting**, page 142, and **Template Cutting**, page 144, to cut fabric.*

1. **From cream solid:** ☐
   - Cut 5 **rectangles** 13" x 23" for triangle-squares.
   - Cut 9 **strips** 2¾"w.
   - Cut 17 **wide strips** 4"w.
   - Cut 4 strips 4¾"w. From these strips, cut 30 squares 4¾" x 4¾". Cut squares twice diagonally to make 120 **triangles**.

2. **From navy print:** ■
   - Cut 5 **rectangles** 13" x 23" for triangle-squares.
   - Cut 7 **strips** 2¾"w.
   - Cut 34 **narrow strips** 1½"w.
   - Cut 60 **A's** using **Template A** pattern, page 76.
   - Cut 30 **B's** using **Template B** pattern, page 76.

ASSEMBLING THE QUILT TOP
*Follow **Piecing and Pressing**, page 144, to make quilt top.*

1. To make triangle-squares, place 1 navy and 1 cream **rectangle** right sides together. Referring to **Fig. 1**, follow **Making Triangle-Squares**, page 145, to make 16 **triangle-squares**. Repeat with remaining **rectangles** to make a total of 80 **triangle-squares**.

Fig. 1

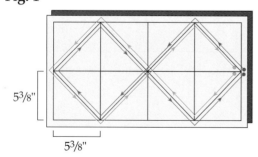

5⅜"

5⅜"

triangle-square (make 80)

2. Sew 2 **strips** together to make **Strip Set A**. Make 3 **Strip Set A's**. Cut across **Strip Set A's** at 2¾" intervals to make 40 **Unit 1's**.

Strip Set A (make 3)   **Unit 1** (make 40)

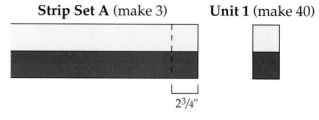

2¾"

3. Sew 5 **strips** together to make **Strip Set B**. Make 2 **Strip Set B's**. Cut across **Strip Set B's** at 2¾" intervals to make 20 **Unit 2's**.

Strip Set B (make 2)   **Unit 2** (make 20)

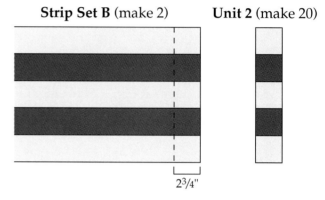

2¾"

4. Sew 2 **triangle-squares** and 1 **Unit 1** together to make **Unit 3**. Make 40 **Unit 3's**.

Unit 3 (make 40)

5. Sew 2 **Unit 3's** and 1 **Unit 2** together to make **Block**. Make 20 **Blocks**.

Block (make 20)

6. Sew 1 **wide** and 2 **narrow strips** together to make **Strip Set C**. Make 17 **Strip Set C's**. Cut across **Strip Set C's** at 11³/₄" intervals to make 49 **Sashing Units**.

Strip Set C (make 17)   **Sashing Unit** (make 49)

11³/₄"

7. Sew 2 **triangles** and 1 **A** together to make **Unit 4**. Make 60 **Unit 4's**.

Unit 4 (make 60)

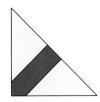

8. Sew 2 **Unit 4's** and 1 **B** together to make **Sashing Square**. Make 30 **Sashing Squares**.

Sashing Square (make 30)

9. Sew 5 **Sashing Squares** and 4 **Sashing Units** together to make **Sashing Row**. Make 6 **Sashing Rows**.

Sashing Row (make 6)

10. Sew 5 **Sashing Units** and 4 **Blocks** together to make **Row**. Make 5 **Rows**.

Row (make 5)

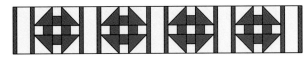

11. Referring to **Quilt Top Diagram**, sew **Sashing Rows** and **Rows** together to complete **Quilt Top**.

COMPLETING THE QUILT

1. Follow **Quilting**, page 149, to mark, layer, and quilt, using **Quilting Diagram** as a suggestion. Our quilt is hand quilted.
2. Cut a 31" square of binding fabric. Follow **Binding**, page 153, to bind quilt using 2¹/₂"w bias binding with mitered corners.

Quilting Diagram

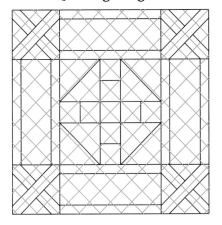

Quilt Top Diagram

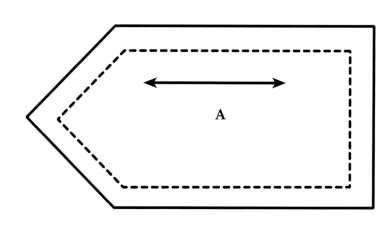

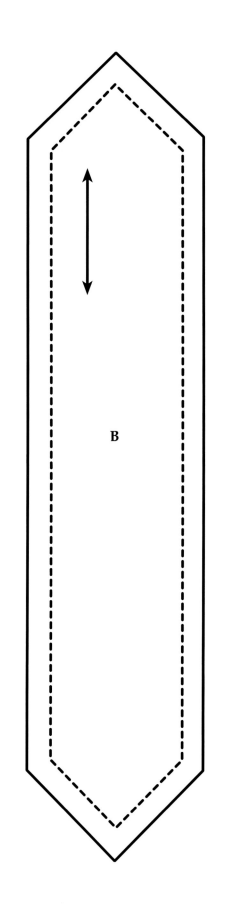

QUICK TIP

ORGANIZING YOUR QUILTMAKING

Using our quick methods makes quiltmaking faster and easier, as well as more enjoyable and satisfying. Organizing your supplies and workspace will help you to accomplish even more during the time you have to devote to quiltmaking. Try the following suggestions:

- *If you don't have a sewing room, use a portable, easily stored container to keep all your tools and supplies in one place. You can use laundry baskets that can be stacked in a closet, under-bed storage boxes, or even a cardboard box stored under a skirted table.*

- *Store all the materials for an individual project in a smaller box or other container. Include the fabric, thread, and other supplies, as well as the project instructions and any special tools or materials you may need. Label the individual project boxes.*

- *Before putting a project away, label any pieces that may be difficult to identify later. Make notes on your instructions (use self-stick notes if you don't want to write in your books) that will help you quickly pick up where you left off.*

- *Never put away a project when you're having a problem. Rip out mistakes and work out problems before you stop working so that you'll look forward to getting back to the project.*

- *Invest in tools and supplies that will make your work easier. Trying to work with poor-quality tools or the wrong tool for the job will only lead to frustration and dissatisfaction with the results.*

- *Choose projects carefully. Alternate quilts that challenge your time and abilities with simpler, smaller projects like wall hangings or lap quilts. Include fast, fun projects that you can finish quickly. The satisfaction of finishing one project is always good motivation to finish another!*

77

CRAZY ABOUT BLUE COLLECTION

As Queen Victoria filled Windsor Castle with her genteel mementos, she inspired an extravagant style that epitomized the late 1800's. Sentimental Victorians devoted themselves to the decorative — lavishing their homes with ornate trinkets and fancy needlework. One favored pastime for proper ladies of the day was an elaborate patchwork form called crazy quilting. A tribute to that romantic era, our Crazy About Blue wall hanging is made by randomly sewing fabrics and edgings to a muslin square and rotary cutting the pieces to size. The assembled blocks are adorned with buttons, lacy appliqués, silk ribbon embroidery, and other trims. For a nostalgic touch, include vintage materials that will bring to mind your own precious memories.

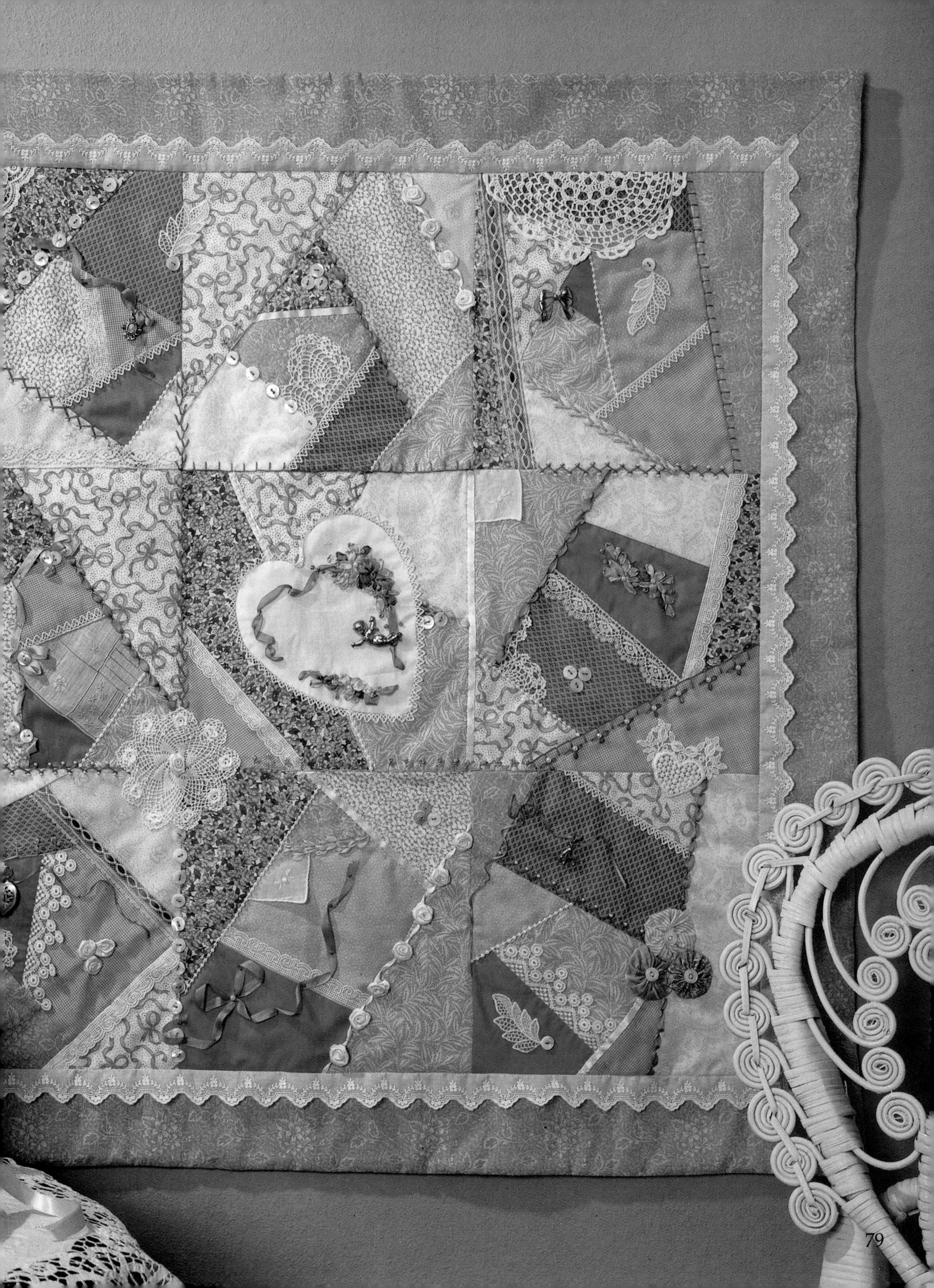

elcome guests in elegant Victorian style with this array of crazy-quilt accessories. Heartwarming accents, our ruffled throw pillows (below) are enhanced with lovely embroidery, ribbons, and lace. The heart motif also appears on a winsome tea cozy (opposite), which is a decorative teapot warmer. Its embellishments include golden charms and old-fashioned fabric yo-yos. A lace-trimmed coaster completes the ensemble.

CRAZY ABOUT BLUE WALL HANGING

SKILL LEVEL: 1 2 3 4 5
BLOCK SIZE: 9" x 9"
WALL HANGING SIZE: 33" x 33"

YARDAGE REQUIREMENTS

Yardage is based on 45"w fabric.

2 yds of blue print for border, backing, and hanging sleeve

2 yds **total** of assorted blue and white print scraps

1 yd of muslin for foundations

1 square 9" x 9" of white solid

$4^1/_8$ yds of 1"w embroidered lace for border

35" x 35" batting

You will also need:

items and trims for embellishment (we used embroidery floss, silk ribbon, pieces of lace and ribbon, beads, buttons, charms, fabric yo-yos, and doilies)

CUTTING OUT THE PIECES

All measurements include a 1/4" seam allowance. Follow Rotary Cutting, page 142, to cut fabric.

1. **From blue print:**
   - Cut 4 **borders** $3^3/_4$" x 37".
   - Cut 1 **backing** 35" x 35".
   - Cut 1 **hanging sleeve** 7" x 33".

2. **From muslin:**
   - Cut 3 strips 9"w. From these strips, cut 9 **foundation squares** 9" x 9".

PIECING THE BLOCKS

1. From 1 of the fabric scraps, cut a five-sided piece. Place this piece, right side up, on 1 **foundation square** (**Fig. 1**).

Fig. 1

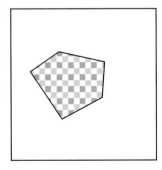

2. Referring to **Figs. 2** and **3**, place a second piece on the first, matching right sides and one straight raw edge. Stitch 1/4" from matched raw edges, stitching through all layers. Flip second piece to right side and press.

Fig. 2

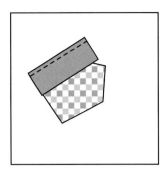

Fig. 3

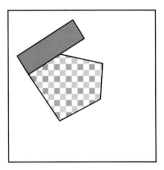

3. Referring to **Figs. 4 - 12**, continue to add pieces, stitch, flip, and press until pieces extend at least 1/4" past all edges of **foundation square**.

Fig. 4

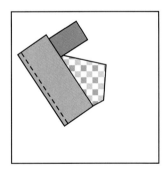

Fig. 5

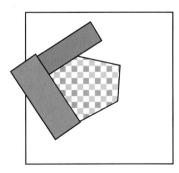

Fig. 6

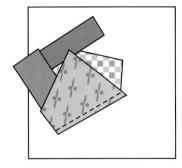

82

Fig. 7

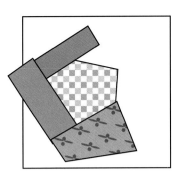

Fig. 8

Fig. 9

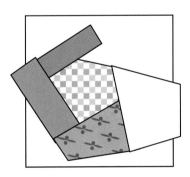

Fig. 10

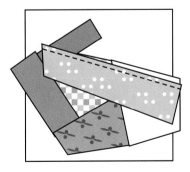

Fig. 11

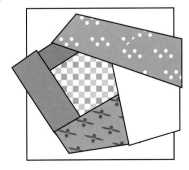

Fig. 12

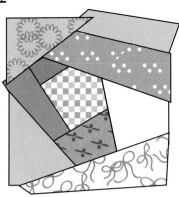

4. Place pieced square, right side down, on cutting mat. Use rotary cutter and ruler to trim off crazy piecing ¼" outside **foundation square** (**Fig. 13**) to complete **Block**.

Fig. 13

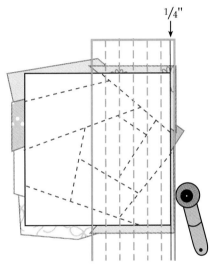

5. Repeat Steps 1 - 4 to make a total of 9 **Blocks**.

Block (make 9)

EMBELLISHING THE BLOCKS

Refer to photo and use the following suggestions to embellish the pieced blocks.

- Using pattern, page 87, trace **Small Heart** outline on white solid square. Using **Embroidery Diagram**, page 87, as a suggestion, follow **Embroidery Stitches**, page 156, to embroider heart. Cut out heart 1/4" outside drawn line. Press 1/4" seam allowance to wrong side. Use blindstitch to appliqué heart to center of one pieced block. Hand or machine stitch narrow lace around edge of heart.
- Use embroidery floss and/or silk ribbon and follow **Embroidery Stitches**, page 156, to add embroidery to seamlines or individual patches.
- Machine or hand stitch lace, ribbon, or other trim along seamlines. Use seam ripper to remove a few stitches at end of adjoining seamline; insert raw end of trim into opening. Blindstitch opening closed.
- Sew on buttons, charms, and beads.
- Use small pieces of crochet or tatting (doilies or sections salvaged from worn pieces), enclosing any cut edges in a seamline to prevent raveling.
- To make each fabric yo-yo, cut a 3½" dia. circle from desired fabric. Turn raw edge of circle 1/4" to wrong side. Using a double strand of quilting thread, work a **Running Stitch**, page 157, along turned edge. Pull ends of thread to tightly gather circle; knot thread securely and trim ends. Flatten circle. Sew on yo-yos, either by stitching through a button in the center of yo-yo or by blindstitching edges to block.

ASSEMBLING THE WALL HANGING TOP

*Follow **Piecing and Pressing**, page 144, to make wall hanging top.*

1. Sew 3 **Blocks** together to make row. Make 3 rows. Sew rows together to complete center section of wall hanging.
2. Cut lace for border into 4 equal pieces. Matching long raw edge of lace to one long raw edge of **border**, baste 1 piece of lace, right side up, to right side of 1 **border**. Repeat with remaining lace pieces and **borders**.
3. Follow **Adding Mitered Borders**, page 148, to sew borders to center section to complete **Wall Hanging Top**.

COMPLETING THE WALL HANGING

1. Center backing fabric, right side up, on batting. With right sides together, center wall hanging top on backing. Working from center outward, smooth out any wrinkles and use safety pins to pin layers together approximately every 6". Use straight pins to pin edges of layers together. Trim batting and backing to same size as wall hanging top.

2. Using a 1/2" seam allowance and leaving a 12" opening for turning, sew layers together. Trim corners, remove all pins, and turn wall hanging right side out. Sew final closure by hand.
3. To quilt wall hanging, refer to **Quilting**, page 149, to hand or machine quilt in the ditch between blocks and around inside edge of border.
4. Add additional embellishment to seamlines between blocks, if desired.
5. Press short edges of **hanging sleeve** 1/4" to wrong side. Press 1/4" to wrong side again and stitch along first fold. Matching right sides and raw edges, stitch 1/4" from raw edges to form a tube. Turn right side out and press.
6. Center sleeve 1" below top edge of wall hanging back. Hand stitch both long edges to wall hanging backing, taking care not to stitch through to front of wall hanging.

Wall Hanging Top Diagram

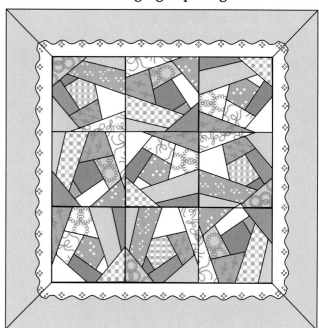

CRAZY HEART PILLOW

PILLOW SIZE: 11" x 13" (including ruffle)

SUPPLIES

9" x 9" piece of muslin for **foundation square**
scraps of blue and white print fabrics
9" x 9" square for pillow back
4½" x 66" fabric strip (pieced as necessary) for ruffle
items and trims for embellishment (we used embroidery floss, silk ribbon, pieces of lace and ribbon, beads, buttons, charms, and doilies)
polyester fiberfill
tracing paper

MAKING THE PILLOW

1. Using foundation square and fabric scraps, follow **Piecing the Blocks**, page 82, to make 1 **Block**.
2. To make pattern for **Pillow Top**, fold tracing paper in half. Place fold on grey line of **Large Heart** pattern, page 86; trace. Cut out pattern; unfold. Position pattern on **Block**; draw around pattern. Do not cut out.
3. Refer to **Embellishing the Blocks**, page 84, to embellish **Block** within the drawn heart shape as desired.
4. Cut out **Pillow Top** 1/2" outside drawn heart shape.
5. Follow **Pillow Finishing**, page 155, to finish pillow with ruffle.

CRAZY FLANGED PILLOW

PILLOW SIZE: 13" x 13" (including flange)

SUPPLIES

9" x 9" piece of muslin for **foundation square**
scraps of blue and white print fabrics
9" x 9" square of white fabric for heart appliqué
1 yd of narrow lace
4 strips 2" x 16" of blue print for pillow top **borders**
1 1/8 yds of 1"w embroidered lace
13 1/2" x 13 1/2" square of fabric for **pillow back**
items and trims for embellishment (we used embroidery floss, silk ribbon, pieces of lace and ribbon, beads, buttons, charms, and doilies)
polyester fiberfill

MAKING THE PILLOW

1. Using **foundation square** and fabric scraps, follow **Piecing the Blocks**, page 82, to make 1 **Block**.
2. Refer to **Embellishing the Blocks**, page 84, to add heart appliqué and other embellishments to **Block** as desired.
3. Follow Steps 3 and 4 of **Assembling the Wall Hanging Top**, page 84, to add **borders** to **Block** to complete **Pillow Top**.
4. Place **Pillow Top** and **pillow back** right sides together. Leaving an opening for turning, stitch 1/4" from raw edge. Clip corners; turn right side out.
5. Leaving a 2"w opening on same side as opening for turning, stitch in the ditch between **Block** and border (**Fig. 1**). Stuff pillow with fiberfill. Sew both openings closed.

Fig. 1

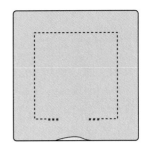

TEA COZY AND COASTER

SUPPLIES

2 rectangles 15" x 20" of blue print fabric
2 rectangles 15" x 20 of lining fabric
2 rectangles 15" x 20" of batting
2 squares 4 1/2" x 4 1/2" of blue print fabric
1 square 4 1/2" x 4 1/2" of batting
1 yd of 2 1/2"w bias fabric strip for binding
items and trims for embellishment (we used embroidery floss, silk ribbon, pieces of lace and ribbon, beads, buttons, charms, and doilies)
tracing paper

MAKING THE TEA COZY AND COASTER

1. To make pattern for tea cozy, fold tracing paper in half. Place fold on grey line of pattern, page 86; trace. Cut out pattern; unfold.
2. Use pattern to cut two pieces each from blue print fabric, lining fabric, and batting.
3. To make cozy front, place 1 blue print piece right side up on 1 batting piece; baste close to edges. Refer to photo and **Embellishing the Blocks**, page 84, to embellish cozy front as desired.
4. To assemble cozy front and lining, match edges and place 1 lining piece and cozy front right sides together. Using a 1/2" seam allowance, stitch through all layers along bottom edges only. Turn right side out and press. Using remaining fabric and batting pieces, repeat to make cozy back.
5. With lining sides facing, place cozy front and back together; baste all layers together along raw edges.
6. Use bias fabric strip and follow Steps 4 and 5 of **Attaching Binding with Overlapped Corners**, page 154, to bind raw edges of tea cozy.
7. To make coaster, place 1 fabric square on batting square to make coaster top. Referring to **Embellishing the Blocks**, page 84, embellish coaster top as desired.
8. Place coaster top and remaining fabric square wrong sides together; baste along raw edges.
9. Use bias fabric strip and follow **Attaching Binding with Mitered Corners**, page 154, to bind coaster.

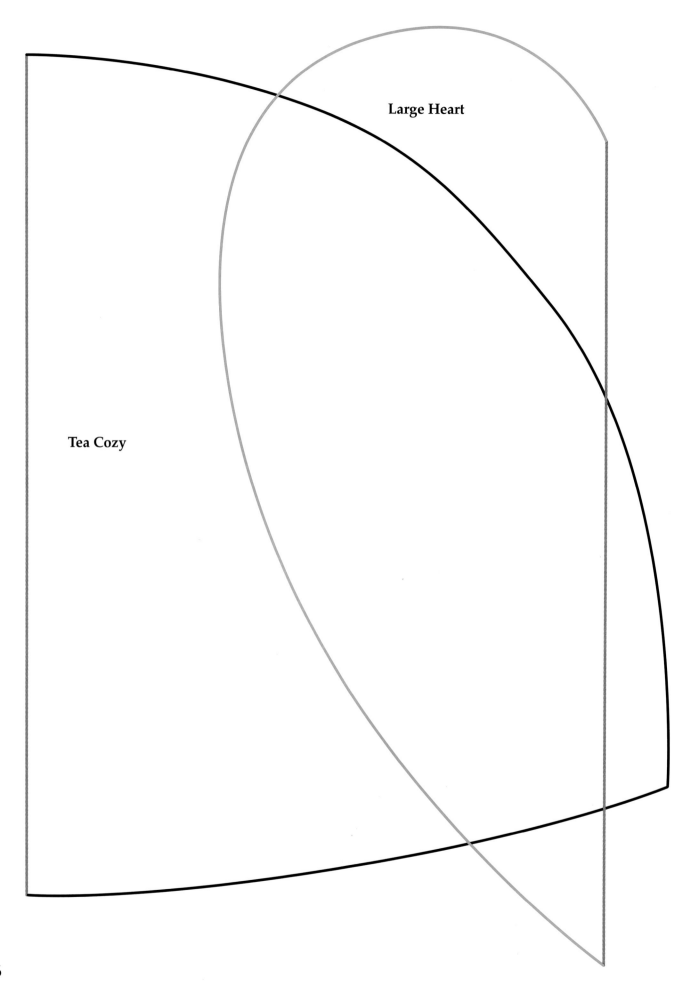

Large Heart

Tea Cozy

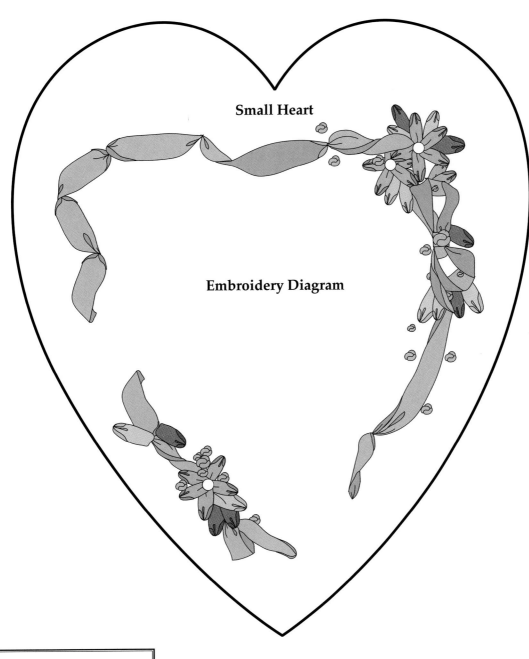

Small Heart

Embroidery Diagram

STITCH KEY

 French Knot

 Japanese Ribbon Stitch

HOUR-GLASSES & GEESE

Time will surely fly while you're having fun piecing this impressive quilt! It's a delightful combination of bold Hourglass blocks set with Flying Geese sashing for a spectacle of pieced triangles. To make the quilt blocks, we used a quick triangle-square method that produces two units at a time. Another easy process, our "sew and flip" technique is a fast and accurate way to create precise points for the Flying Geese units. The design is complemented with basic echo quilting, and the edges are simply finished with plain bias binding.

HOURGLASSES AND GEESE QUILT

SKILL LEVEL: 1 2 3 4 5
BLOCK SIZE: 8¼" x 8¼"
QUILT SIZE: 81" x 92"

YARDAGE REQUIREMENTS
Yardage is based on 45"w fabric.

 6⅞ yds of cream print
 6⅛ yds of blue solid
7½ yds for backing
1 yd for binding
90" x 108" batting

CUTTING OUT THE PIECES
All measurements include a ¼" seam allowance. Follow
Rotary Cutting, page 142, to cut fabric.

1. **From cream print:**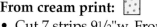
    *   Cut 7 strips 9½"w. From these strips, cut 28 **squares** 9½" x 9½".

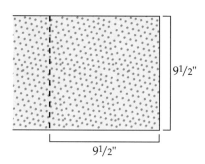

square (cut 28)

9½"

9½"

*   Cut 83 strips 1⅞"w. From these strips, cut 1,812 **small squares** 1⅞" x 1⅞".

small square
(cut 1,812)

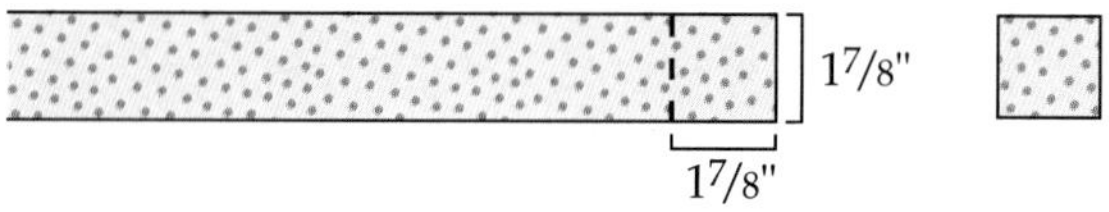

1⅞"

1⅞"

2. **From blue solid:**
    *   Cut 7 strips 9½"w. From these strips, cut 28 **squares** 9½" x 9½".

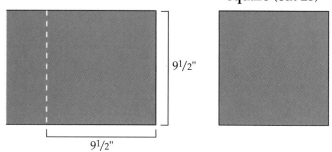

square (cut 28)

9½"

9½"

90

*   Cut 42 strips 3¼"w. From these strips, cut 906 **rectangles** 1⅞" x 3¼".

rectangle
(cut 906)

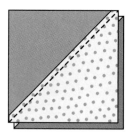

3¼"

1⅞"

ASSEMBLING THE QUILT TOP
*Follow **Piecing and Pressing**, page 144, to make quilt top.*

1. To make triangle-squares, place 1 blue and 1 cream **square** right sides together. On wrong side of cream square, draw a diagonal line in one direction; stitch ¼" from each side of line (**Fig. 1**). Cut apart on drawn line to make 2 **triangle-squares**. Press open, pressing seam allowance toward darker fabric. Repeat with remaining squares to make a total of 56 **triangle-squares**.

Fig. 1

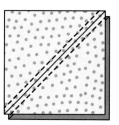

triangle-square (make 56)

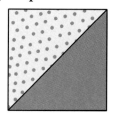

2. Referring to **Fig. 2**, place 2 **triangle-squares** right sides and opposite colors together, matching seams. Referring to **Fig. 3**, draw a diagonal line. Stitch ¼" from each side of line. Cut apart on drawn line and press open to make 2 **Blocks**. Repeat with remaining **triangle-squares** to make a total of 56 **Blocks**.

Fig. 2

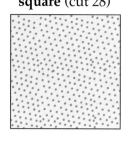

Fig. 3

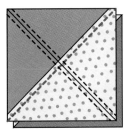

Block (make 56)

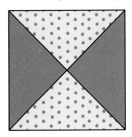

3. Place 1 **small square** on 1 **rectangle** and stitch diagonally as shown in **Fig. 4**. Trim ¼" from stitching line as shown in **Fig. 5**. Press open, pressing seam allowance toward darker fabric.

Fig. 4

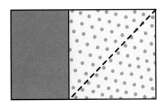

Fig. 5

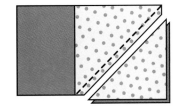

4. Place 1 **small square** on opposite end of **rectangle**. Stitch diagonally as shown in **Fig. 6**. Trim ¼" from stitching line as shown in **Fig. 7**. Press open, pressing seam allowance toward darker fabric to make **Unit 1**.

Fig. 6

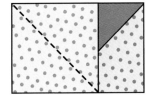

Fig. 7

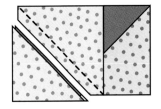

Unit 1

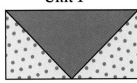

5. Repeat Steps 3 and 4 using remaining **small squares** and **rectangles** to make a total of 906 **Unit 1's**.
6. Sew 6 **Unit 1's** together to make **Sashing Unit**. Make 127 **Sashing Units**.

Sashing Unit (make 127)

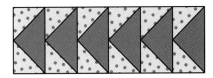

7. Sew 2 **Unit 1's** together to make **Sashing Square**. Make 72 **Sashing Squares**.

Sashing Square (make 72)

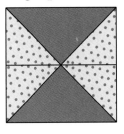

8. Sew 8 **Sashing Squares** and 7 **Sashing Units** together to make **Sashing Row**. Make 9 **Sashing Rows**.
9. Sew 8 **Sashing Units** and 7 **Blocks** together to make **Row**. Make 8 **Rows**.
10. Referring to **Quilt Top Diagram**, page 93, sew **Sashing Rows** and **Rows** together to complete **Quilt Top**.

COMPLETING THE QUILT

1. Follow **Quilting**, page 149, to mark, layer, and quilt, using **Quilting Diagram** as a suggestion. Our quilt is hand quilted.
2. Cut a 32" square of binding fabric. Follow **Binding**, page 153, to bind quilt using 2½"w bias binding with mitered corners.

Sashing Row (make 9)

Row (make 8)

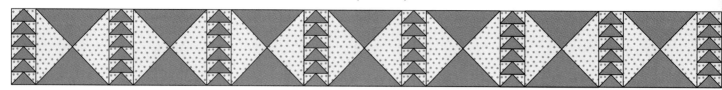

Quilting Diagram

JACOB'S LADDER COLLECTION

Familiar stories from the Bible provided a wealth of inspiration for early quilters. This influence is reflected in the titles of many classic patterns we love today. One such design, known as Jacob's Ladder, was named for the vision in which God revealed his covenant with the children of Israel. Arranged in a straight-furrows setting, the contrasting squares of our quilt represent the angel-trod steps from heaven that appeared in Jacob's dream. The design is simple to create using easy grid-pieced triangle-squares and strip-set units. A plain outer border finishes the quilt with a divinely soft edge.

Traditional ticking-style fabric enhances the cheerful look of our old-fashioned window accents (opposite). The cleverly designed shade is raised and lowered by adjusting the pretty ticking ties. Featuring a border of Jacob's Ladder units, the valance is edged with easy prairie points. Just right for quiet moments, this comfy bathrobe (below) is embellished with striped fabric and prairie-point trim.

JACOB'S LADDER QUILT

SKILL LEVEL: 1 2 3 4 5
BLOCK SIZE: 12" x 12"
QUILT SIZE: 93" x 105"

YARDAGE REQUIREMENTS

Yardage is based on 45"w fabric.

☐ 7¼ yds of white print
■ 5¾ yds of navy print
8½ yds for backing
1 yd for binding
120" x 120" batting

CUTTING OUT THE PIECES

All measurements include a ¼" seam allowance. Follow Rotary Cutting, page 142, to cut fabric.

1. **From white print:** ☐
    - Cut 43 **strips** 2"w.
    - Cut 2 lengthwise **side borders** 4½" x 112".
    - Cut 2 lengthwise **top/bottom borders** 4½" x 100".
    - Cut 9 **squares** 21" x 21" for triangle-squares.

2. **From navy print:** ■
    - Cut 43 **strips** 2"w.
    - Cut 9 **squares** 21" x 21" for triangle-squares.

ASSEMBLING THE QUILT TOP

Follow Piecing and Pressing, page 144, to make quilt top.

1. Sew 2 **strips** together to make **Strip Set**. Make 43 **Strip Sets**. Cut across **Strip Sets** at 2" intervals to make 896 **Unit 1's**.

Strip Set (make 43)   **Unit 1** (cut 896)

2"

2. Sew 2 **Unit 1's** together to make **Unit 2**. Make 448 **Unit 2's**.

Unit 2 (make 448)

3. To make **triangle-squares**, place 1 white and 1 navy **square** right sides together. Referring to **Fig. 1**, follow **Making Triangle-Squares**, page 145, to make 50 **triangle-squares**. Repeat with remaining **squares** to make a total of 450 **triangle-squares**. (You will need 448 and have 2 left over.)

Fig. 1

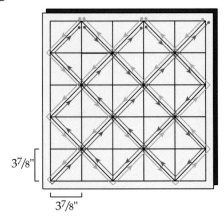

3⅞"

3⅞"

triangle-square (make 450)

4. Sew 2 **triangle-squares** and 2 **Unit 2's** together to make **Unit 3**. Make 112 **Unit 3's**.

Unit 3 (make 112)

5. Sew 2 **triangle-squares** and 2 **Unit 2's** together to make **Unit 4**. Make 112 **Unit 4's**.

Unit 4 (make 112)

6. Sew 2 **Unit 3's** and 2 **Unit 4's** together to make **Block**. Make 56 **Blocks**.

Block (make 56)

7. Sew 7 **Blocks** together to make **Row**. Make 8 **Rows**.

Row (make 8)

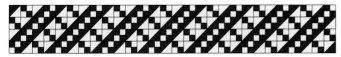

8. Referring to **Quilt Top Diagram**, sew **Rows** together to make center section of quilt top.
9. Follow **Adding Mitered Borders**, page 148, to add **borders** to center section to complete **Quilt Top**.

COMPLETING THE QUILT

1. Follow **Quilting**, page 149, to mark, layer, and quilt. Our quilt is quilted in the ditch by hand.
2. Cut a 34" square of binding fabric. Follow **Binding**, page 153, to bind quilt using 2¹/₂"w bias binding with mitered corners.

Quilt Top Diagram

PRAIRIE POINT BATHROBE

SUPPLIES
robe with shawl collar
1 yd of 45"w navy striped fabric
³/₄ yd of 45"w navy solid fabric
1 yd of ¹/₄" dia. cord for welting

TRIMMING THE ROBE

1. Wash, dry, and press robe and fabrics.
2. Measure outer edge of shawl collar. Cut 2"w bias strip of striped fabric 1" longer than determined measurement, piecing as necessary. Press 1 long edge of bias strip ¹/₄" to wrong side; press both short edges ¹/₂" to wrong side.
3. To determine number of prairie points needed for collar, divide measurement determined in Step 2 by 2¹/₂, rounding up to next whole number. Cut the determined number of 3" x 3" squares of navy solid fabric.
4. To make prairie points, fold each square in half diagonally with wrong sides together; fold in half again and press (**Fig. 1**).

Fig. 1

5. Aligning raw edges of prairie points with edge of collar, arrange prairie points evenly along underside of collar (**Fig. 2**).

Fig. 2

6. Arrange bias fabric strip, right side down, over prairie points, aligning long raw edge with edge of collar. Pin or baste in place. Machine stitch through all layers ¹/₄" from edges.
7. Fold bias fabric strip to right side of collar and press. Blindstitch folded edges to collar.
8. For each pocket trim, measure along top edge of pocket. Cut 1¹/₂"w bias strip of striped fabric 1" longer than determined length. Press 1 long raw edge of bias strip ¹/₄" to wrong side; press both short edges ¹/₂" to wrong side.

9. Follow Steps 3 and 4 to determine number and make prairie points for pocket trim. Arrange prairie points along raw edge of bias strip, matching raw edges. Machine stitch through all layers ¼" from raw edges (**Fig. 3**). Fold prairie points down; press seam allowance toward bias strip to make pocket trim.

Fig. 3

10. Position trim at top of pocket; blindstitch edges to pocket.
11. For each cuff trim, measure edge of cuff. Cut 1½"w bias strip of striped fabric 1" longer than determined measurement. Cut 2"w bias strip of navy solid fabric and ¼" dia. cord, each 2" longer than determined measurement.
12. To make welting, lay cord along center of navy solid bias strip on wrong side of fabric; fold strip over cord. Using a zipper foot, machine baste along length of strip close to cord. Trim seam allowance to ¼".
13. Using a ½" seam allowance, sew short raw edges of striped bias fabric strip together to form trim band. Matching right sides and raw edges and beginning and ending 3" from ends of welting, baste welting to one raw edge of trim band.
14. Remove approximately 3" of seam at 1 end of welting; fold fabric away from cord. Trim remaining end of welting so that cord ends meet exactly (**Fig. 4**). Fold short edge of welting fabric ½" to wrong side; fold fabric back over area where ends meet (**Fig. 5**); baste in place. Stitch welting to trim band close to cord; remove basting threads.

Fig. 4   **Fig. 5**

15. Matching right side of trim band to wrong side of cuff and aligning raw edge of trim band to edge of cuff, pin or baste trim in place. Machine stitch trim to cuff ¼" from raw edge. Fold trim to right side of cuff and press. Using a zipper foot, machine stitch in the ditch between welting and trim band.

PRAIRIE POINT VALANCE

Our valance will fit a standard 36"w window.

YARDAGE REQUIREMENTS
Yardage is based on 45"w fabric.

⬜ ⅞ yd of white solid for valance and valance lining

⬛ ⅜ yd of navy solid for pieced band and prairie points

⬜ ¼ yd of white print for pieced band

CUTTING OUT THE PIECES
All measurements include a ¼" seam allowance. Follow **Rotary Cutting**, *page 142, to cut fabric.*

1. **From white solid:** ⬜
   - Cut 1 **valance** 10" x 40".
   - Cut 1 **valance lining** 14½" x 40".

2. **From navy solid:** ⬛
   - Cut 1 **strip** 2"w.
   - Cut 2 strips 4¼"w. From this strip, cut 18 **squares** 4¼" x 4¼".

3. **From white print:** ⬜
   - Cut 1 **strip** 2"w.
   - Cut 1 **strip** 5½"w. From this strip, cut 5 squares 5½" x 5½". Cut squares twice diagonally to make 20 **triangles**. (You will need 18 and have 2 left over.)

MAKING THE VALANCE
Follow **Piecing and Pressing**, *page 144, to make valance.*

1. Sew **strips** together to make **Strip Set**. Cut across **Strip Set** at 2" intervals to make 20 **Unit 1's**.

Strip Set   **Unit 1** (make 20)

2. Sew 2 **Unit 1's** together to make **Unit 2**. Make 10 **Unit 2's**.

Unit 2 (make 10)

3. Sew 1 **Unit 2** and 2 **triangles** together to make **Unit 3**. Make 8 **Unit 3's**.

Unit 3 (make 8)

4. Sew 1 **Unit 2** and 1 **triangle** together to make **Unit 4**. Make 2 **Unit 4's**.

Unit 4 (make 2)

5. Sew **Unit 3's** and **Unit 4's** together to make **Pieced Band**.

Pieced Band

6. To trim ends of **Pieced Band**, refer to **Fig. 1** to align 1/4" marking (shown in pink) on rotary cutting ruler with seam intersections. Use rotary cutter to trim away excess fabric.

Fig. 1

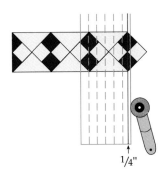

1/4"

7. To make prairie points, fold **squares** in half diagonally with wrong sides together; fold in half again and press (see **Fig. 1**, page 99). Repeat to make a total of 18 **prairie points**.
8. With right sides together, arrange 9 **prairie points** along one long raw edge of **Pieced Band**, overlapping as necessary. Pin or baste in place. Matching right sides, sew **Pieced Band** and **valance** together, enclosing raw edges of prairie points in seam to make **Valance Top**.
9. With right sides together, arrange remaining 9 **prairie points** along remaining edge of **Pieced Band**, overlapping as necessary. Pin or baste in place. Matching right sides and raw edges and leaving an opening for turning, sew **Valance Top** and **valance lining** together, enclosing raw edges of prairie points in seam.
10. Clip corners and turn **Valance** right side out; press. Sew opening closed by hand.
11. To make rod pocket, press top edge of valance 2" to wrong side; blindstitch long edge in place.

WINDOW SHADE

SUPPLIES
1/2"w flat-mounted sash rod
white solid fabric for shade
navy striped fabric for shade lining and ties
2" dia. cardboard tube

MAKING THE SHADE
1. Mount sash rod at top of window opening.
2. To determine width of shade, measure width of window opening; add 1". To determine length of shade, measure from top of rod to windowsill; add 11".
3. Using the determined measurements, cut one shade piece and one lining piece.
4. Place shade piece and lining piece right sides together. Using a 1/2" seam allowance, sew pieces together along three sides, leaving one short edge open. Clip corners and turn right side out; press.
5. To make rod pocket, fold unsewn (top) edges 1/2" to wrong side. Turn 2" to wrong side again and stitch close to first fold. Hang shade on rod.
6. To make ties, cut two lengthwise pieces of striped fabric 4"w and twice the length of shade, piecing as necessary. Matching right sides and raw edges, fold each piece in half lengthwise. Leaving an opening for turning, use a 1/2" seam allowance to stitch along all raw edges. Trim corners, turn right side out, and press. Stitch opening closed by hand.
7. To roll shade, hang ties over top of shade. Roll bottom of shade toward front onto cardboard tube. Secure shade by tying ends of ties into bows.

BABY BLUE COLLECTION

Perfect for wrapping wee ones in love, the cuddly quilts in this collection will become treasured heirlooms. Our adorable baby bunting quilt provides snuggly warmth for baby, both at home and on the go. The clever quilt is created using grid-pieced triangle-squares and strip-pieced units. Button the sides of the quilt together and close the drawstring edge, and it becomes a cozy bunting! As baby grows older, the quilt can easily be converted to a wall hanging by using the casing as a hanging sleeve.

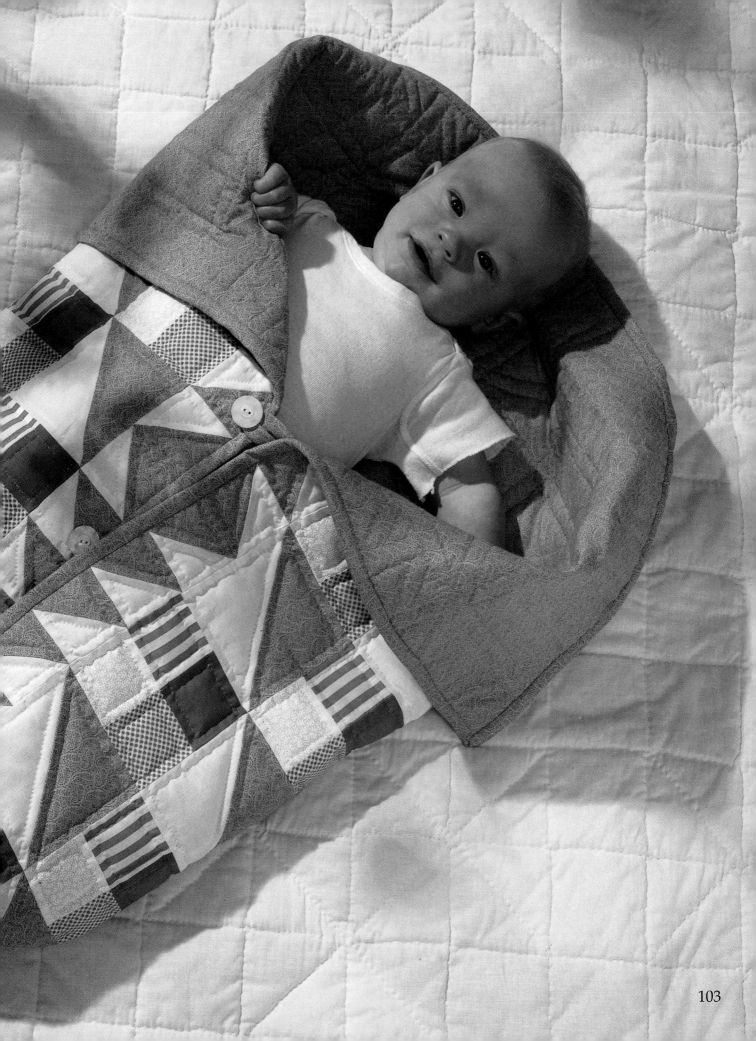

*L*ife is but a dream when little ones are surrounded by the merry sailboats on this nautical
baby quilt (opposite). It also makes a delightful wall hanging! Each block is simple to make
with grid-pieced triangle-squares and plain rectangles. The seagoing effect is enhanced
with quilted "waves." A pretty bouquet of posies graces a quilt for a baby girl (below).
The floral motifs are stitched in place using an easy invisible appliqué technique.

SAILBOAT BABY QUILT

SKILL LEVEL: 1 2 3 4 5
BLOCK SIZE: 10" x 10"
QUILT SIZE: 47" x 72"

To bring our vintage 1960's Sailboat quilt more in line with today's quick methods and standards, our instructions include simplified piecing and more durable double-fold binding.

YARDAGE REQUIREMENTS
Yardage is based on 45"w fabric.

- 2⁷/₈ yds of blue solid
- 1³/₄ yds of white solid
  3¹/₈ yds for backing
  ⁷/₈ yd for binding
  72" x 90" batting

CUTTING OUT THE PIECES
*All measurements include a ¹/₄" seam allowance. Follow **Rotary Cutting**, page 142, to cut fabric.*

1. **From blue solid:**
   - Cut 2 **squares** 19" x 19" for triangle-squares.
   - Cut 2 lengthwise **side borders** 5" x 71¹/₂".
   - Cut 2 lengthwise **sashing strips** 4" x 71¹/₂".
   - From remaining fabric width, cut 3 strips 5¹/₂"w. From these strips, cut 15 **rectangles** 3" x 5¹/₂".
   - Cut 4 strips 10¹/₂"w. From these strips, cut 18 **sashing rectangles** 4" x 10¹/₂".

2. **From white solid:**
   - Cut 2 **squares** 19" x 19" for triangle-squares.
   - Cut 3 strips 5¹/₂"w. From these strips, cut 30 **rectangles** 3" x 5¹/₂".
   - Cut 2 strips 10¹/₂"w. From these strips, cut 15 **large rectangles** 3" x 10¹/₂".

ASSEMBLING THE QUILT TOP
*Follow **Piecing and Pressing**, page 144, to make quilt top.*

1. To make triangle-squares, place 1 blue and 1 white **square** right sides together. Referring to **Fig. 1**, follow **Making Triangle-Squares**, page 145, to make 50 **triangle-squares**. Repeat with remaining **squares** to make a total of 100 **triangle-squares**. (You will need 90 and have 10 left over.)

Fig. 1

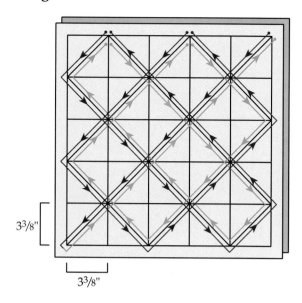

3³/₈"

3³/₈"

triangle-square (make 100)

2. Sew 4 **triangle-squares** together to make **Unit 1**. Make 15 **Unit 1's**.

Unit 1 (make 15)

3. Sew 1 **Unit 1** and 2 **rectangles** together to make **Unit 2**. Make 15 **Unit 2's**.

Unit 2 (make 15)

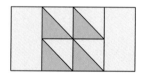

4. Sew 2 **triangle-squares** and 1 **rectangle** together to make **Unit 3**. Make 15 **Unit 3's**.

Unit 3 (make 15)

5. Sew 1 **Unit 2**, 1 **Unit 3**, and 1 **large rectangle** together to make **Block**. Make 15 **Blocks**.

Block (make 15)

6. Sew 6 **sashing rectangles** and 5 **Blocks** together to make 1 vertical **Row**. Make 3 **Rows**.

Row (make 3)

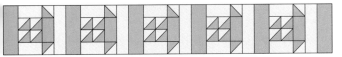

7. Referring to **Quilt Top Diagram**, sew 3 **Rows** and 2 **sashing strips** together to make center section of quilt top.
8. Sew **side borders** to center section to complete **Quilt Top**.

COMPLETING THE QUILT
1. Follow **Quilting**, page 149, to mark, layer, and quilt, using **Quilting Diagram** as a suggestion. Our quilt is hand quilted.
2. Cut a 27" square of binding fabric. Follow **Binding**, page 153, to bind quilt using 2¹/₂"w bias binding with mitered corners.

Quilting Diagram

Quilt Top Diagram

BABY BUNTING QUILT

SKILL LEVEL: 1 2 3 4 5
BLOCK SIZE: 4" x 4"
QUILT SIZE: 41" x 33"

YARDAGE REQUIREMENTS
Yardage is based on 45"w fabric.

1¹/₄ yds *each* of blue print and white solid

¹/₄ yd *each* of blue solid, blue stripe, blue check, and white print
1¹/₂ yds for backing
³/₄ yd for binding
45" x 60" batting

You will also need:
   3 white 1"dia. buttons

CUTTING OUT THE PIECES
*All measurements include a ¹/₄" seam allowance. Follow **Rotary Cutting**, page 142, to cut fabric.*

1. **From blue print:**
   • Cut 2 lengthwise **narrow strips** 1¹/₂" x 45" for drawstring and loops.
   • Cut 1 **large square** 21" x 21" for large triangle-squares.
   • Cut 2 **squares** 13" x 13" for small triangle-squares.
   • Cut 4 **small squares** 2¹/₂" x 2¹/₂".

2. **From white solid:**
   - Cut 1 **large square** 21" x 21" for large triangle-squares.
   - Cut 2 **squares** 13" x 13" for small triangle-squares.

3. **From blue solid, blue stripe, blue check, and white print:**
   - Cut 2 **strips** 2½"w from *each* fabric.

ASSEMBLING THE QUILT TOP

*Follow **Piecing and Pressing**, page 144, to make quilt top.*

1. To make large triangle-squares, place blue print and white solid **large squares** right sides together. Referring to **Fig. 1**, follow **Making Triangle-Squares**, page 145, to make 32 large triangle-squares for **Block A's**. (You will need 31 and have 1 left over.)

Fig. 1

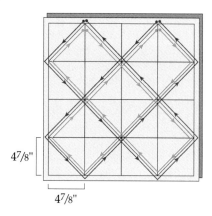

4⁷/₈"

4⁷/₈"

Block A (make 32)

2. Sew **strips** together to make **Strip Set A**. Make 2 **Strip Set A's**. Cut across **Strip Set A's** at 2½" intervals to make 32 **Unit 1's**.

Strip Set A (make 2)   **Unit 1** (make 32)

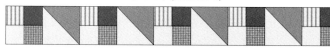

2½"

3. Sew **strips** together to make **Strip Set B**. Make 2 **Strip Set B's**. Cut across **Strip Set B's** at 2½" intervals to make 32 **Unit 2's**.

Strip Set B (make 2)   Unit 2 (make 32)

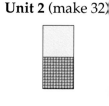

2½"

4. Sew 1 **Unit 1** and 1 **Unit 2** together to make **Block B**. Make 32 **Block B's**.

Block B (make 32)

5. Sew 4 **Block A's** and 5 **Block B's** together to make **Row A**. Make 4 **Row A's**.

Row A (make 4)

6. Sew 5 **Block A's** and 4 **Block B's** together to make **Row B**. Make 3 **Row B's**.

Row B (make 3)

7. Referring to **Bunting Top Diagram**, sew **Row A's** and **Row B's** together to make center section of bunting top.

8. To make small triangle-squares, place 1 blue print and 1 white solid **square** together. Referring to **Fig. 2**, follow **Making Triangle-Squares**, page 145, to make 32 **small triangle-squares**. Repeat with remaining squares to make a total of 64 **small triangle-squares**.

Fig. 2

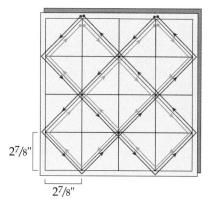

2⁷/₈"

2⁷/₈"

small triangle-square (make 64)

9. Sew 18 **small triangle-squares** and 2 **small squares** together to make **Top/Bottom Border**. Make 2 **Top/Bottom Borders**.

Top/Bottom Border (make 2)

10. Sew 14 **small triangle-squares** together to make **Side Border**. Make 2 **Side Borders**.

Side Border (make 2)

11. Sew **Side**, then **Top** and **Bottom Borders** to center section to complete **Bunting Top**.

COMPLETING THE BUNTING

1. Follow **Quilting**, page 149, to mark, layer, and quilt. Our bunting quilt is outline quilted by hand.
2. To make drawstring casing, cut a piece of backing fabric 3" x 38". Follow Steps 2 - 6 of **Making a Hanging Sleeve**, page 155, to attach casing to 1 long edge of bunting back.
3. To make loops, fold and stitch 1 **narrow strip** lengthwise, matching right sides and raw edges. Stitch 1/4" from long raw edges; turn right side out and press. Cut 3 pieces 3 1/2"l. Fold each piece as shown in **Fig. 3**. Referring to **Bunting Top Diagram** for placement, baste **loops** to **Bunting Top**.

Fig. 3

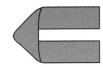

4. Cut a 22" square of binding fabric. Follow **Binding**, page 153, to bind bunting using 2 1/2"w bias binding with mitered corners.
5. Sew buttons securely to bunting edge opposite loops.
6. To make drawstring, fold, stitch, and turn remaining **narrow strip** as in Step 3. Attach safety pin to one end of drawstring and pull through drawstring casing on bunting. Tie a knot at each end of drawstring.

Bunting Top Diagram

VASE OF FLOWERS BABY QUILT

SKILL LEVEL: 1 2 **3** 4 5
QUILT SIZE: 44" x 49"

YARDAGE REQUIREMENTS

Yardage is based on 45"w fabric.

☐ 2¹/₂ yds of white solid
▨ ¹/₂ yd of light blue print
▨ ¹/₂ yd of blue print
▨ ¹/₄ yd of light blue check
▨ ¹/₈ yd of dark blue print
   2³/₄ yds for backing
   ⁵/₈ yd for binding
   45" x 60" batting

You will also need:
   paper-backed fusible web
   transparent monofilament thread

CUTTING OUT THE PIECES

All measurements include a ¹/₄" seam allowance. Follow
***Rotary Cutting**, page 142, to cut fabric.*

1. **From white solid:** ☐
   - Cut 1 **rectangle** 17¹/₂" x 22¹/₂" for medallion background.
   - Cut 2 **side outer borders** 6¹/₂" x 37¹/₂".
   - Cut 2 **top/bottom outer borders** 6¹/₂" x 32¹/₂".
   - Cut 2 **side appliqué panels** 7¹/₂" x 26¹/₂".
   - Cut 2 **top/bottom appliqué panels** 7¹/₂" x 21¹/₂".
   - Cut 8 **corner squares** 6¹/₂" x 6¹/₂".

2. **From light blue print:** ▨
   - Cut 2 **side inner borders** 2" x 25¹/₂".
   - Cut 2 **top/bottom inner borders** 2" x 17¹/₂".

PREPARING THE APPLIQUÉS

*Use patterns, pages 111 and 113, and follow **Preparing
Fusible Appliqués**, page 146, to make appliqués.*

1. **From light blue print:**
   - Cut 25 **flowers**.

2. **From blue print:**
   - Cut 25 **leaves**.
   - Cut 5 **bows**.

3. **From light blue check:**
   - Cut 25 **flower centers**.
   - Cut 1 **vase**.

4. **From dark blue print:**
   - Cut 24 **short stems**.
   - Cut 1 **long stem**.
   - Cut 1 **scallop**.
   - Cut 1 **base**.

ASSEMBLING THE QUILT TOP

*Follow **Piecing and Pressing**, page 144, to make
quilt top.*

1. Reserving **flower centers** and 4 **bows**, refer to **Quilt Top Diagram**, page 112, and follow **Invisible Appliqué**, page 146, to arrange **appliqués** and stitch to **rectangle** and **appliqué panels**.

2. Follow **Satin Stitch Appliqué**, page 148, to stitch 1 **flower center** to each **flower** appliqué.

3. Trim **rectangle** to 17¹/₂" x 22¹/₂". Trim **side appliqué panels** to 6¹/₂" x 25¹/₂"; trim **top/bottom appliqué panels** to 6¹/₂" x 20¹/₂".

4. Sew **top**, **bottom**, then **side inner borders** to **rectangle**.

5. Sew 1 **corner square** to each end of each **side appliqué panel**. Sew **top**, **bottom**, then **side appliqué panels** to **rectangle** to make center section of quilt top.

6. Sew 1 **corner square** to each end of each **side outer border**. Sew **top**, **bottom**, then **side outer borders** to center section.

7. Referring to **Quilt Top Diagram**, follow **Invisible Appliqué**, page 146, to appliqué **bows** to corners to complete **Quilt Top**.

COMPLETING THE QUILT

1. To mark scallops on quilt top edges, refer to **Fig. 1** and mark dots 1¹/₂" from edge of quilt top at 5" intervals. Use a compass or round object to draw scalloped lines connecting dots. Do not trim.

Fig. 1

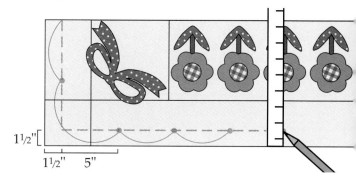

2. Follow **Quilting**, page 149, to mark, layer, and quilt, using **Quilting Diagram** as a suggestion. Our quilt is hand quilted.

3. Cut an 18" square of binding fabric. Follow **Making Continuous Bias Strip Binding**, page 153, to make approximately 6 yds of 1⁵/₈"w bias binding.

4. Following Steps 1 and 2 of **Attaching Binding with Mitered Corners**, page 154, pin binding to front of quilt, matching raw edges of binding to scalloped line. Using a ¼" seam allowance and easing around curves, sew binding to quilt until binding overlaps beginning end by 2"; trim excess binding. Trim quilt top, batting, and backing even with raw edges of binding. Fold binding over to quilt backing and pin in place, covering stitching line. Blindstitch binding to backing.

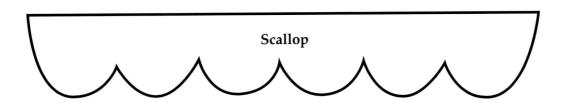

Short Stem

Base

Long Stem

Scallop

Quilting Diagram

Bow

Flower

Flower
Center

Leaves

Vase

DUTCH WINDMILL

The Dutch Windmill design was among the hundreds of patterns featured in newspapers during the 1920's and '30's. Columns about quilting were widely read and made it possible to introduce designs to quilters in all areas of the country at once. For Depression-era stitchers, those newspapers quickly became an invaluable — and inexpensive — resource. For our version of this design, we simplified traditional piecing methods by using grid-pieced units to create two basic blocks. Round motifs are cut from the smaller blocks using simple templates. Those motifs are then appliquéd in place over larger matching blocks, forming the fascinating geometric look.

DUTCH WINDMILL QUILT

SKILL LEVEL: 1 2 3 4 5
BLOCK SIZE: 10" x 10"
QUILT SIZE: 71" x 81"

YARDAGE REQUIREMENTS

Yardage is based on 45"w fabric.

- ■ 6½ yds of navy print
- □ 6½ yds of white solid
- 2⅝ yds of organdy or other very lightweight cotton fabric
- 5 yds for backing
- 1 yd for binding
- 81" x 96" batting

You will also need:
- translucent template material
- fine-point permanent pen
- fabric marking pencil
- pinking shears
- transparent monofilament thread

CUTTING OUT THE PIECES

All measurements include a ¼" seam allowance. Follow Rotary Cutting, page 142, to cut fabric.

1. **From navy print:** ■
   - Cut 2 lengthwise **side outer borders** 2¾" x 80".
   - Cut 2 lengthwise **top/bottom outer borders** 2¾" x 74".
   - Cut 14 **rectangle A's** 13" x 19" for triangle-square A's.
   - Cut 6 **rectangle B's** 12" x 20" for triangle-square B's.
   - Cut 6 **rectangle C's** 15" x 23" for triangle-square C's.

2. **From white solid:** □
   - Cut 2 lengthwise **side inner borders** 3" x 75".
   - Cut 2 lengthwise **top/bottom inner borders** 3" x 70".
   - Cut 14 **rectangle A's** 13" x 19" for triangle-square A's.
   - Cut 6 **rectangle B's** 12" x 20" for triangle-square B's.
   - Cut 6 **rectangle C's** 15" x 23" for triangle-square C's.

3. **From organdy:**
   - Cut 6 strips 5½"w. From these strips, cut 42 **large squares** 5½" x 5½".
   - Cut 14 strips 3½"w. From these strips, cut 168 **small squares** 3½" x 3½".

ASSEMBLING THE QUILT TOP

*Use patterns, page 118, and follow Step 1 of **Template Cutting**, page 144, to make **Templates A** and **B**. Follow Piecing and Pressing, page 144, to make quilt top.*

1. To make triangle-square A's, place 1 navy and 1 white **rectangle A** right sides together. Referring to **Fig. 1**, follow **Making Triangle-Squares**, page 145, to make 12 **triangle-square A's**. Repeat with remaining **rectangle A's** to make a total of 168 **triangle-square A's**.

Fig. 1

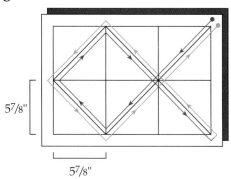

5⅞"

5⅞"

triangle-square A (make 168)

2. Sew 4 **triangle-square A's** together to make **Unit** Make 42 **Unit 1's**.

Unit 1 (make 42)

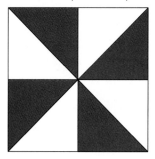

3. To make triangle-square B's, place 1 navy and 1 white **rectangle B** right sides together. Referrin to **Fig. 2**, follow **Making Triangle-Squares**, page 145, to make 30 **triangle-square B's**. Repeat with remaining **rectangle B's** to make a total of 180 **triangle-square B's**. (You will need 168 and have 12 left over.)

Fig. 2

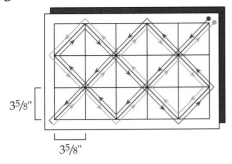

$3^5/8"$

$3^5/8"$

triangle-square B (make 180)

4. Sew 4 **triangle-square B's** together to make **Unit 2**. Make 42 **Unit 2's**.

Unit 2 (make 42)

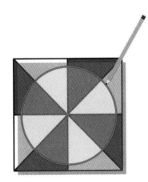

5. Place 1 **Unit 2** and 1 organdy **large square** right sides together. Use center dot and lines to center **template A** on wrong side of organdy square; use pencil to draw around template (**Fig. 3**).

Fig. 3

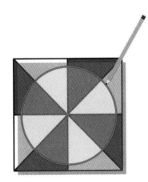

6. Stitch on drawn line. Use pinking shears to trim seam allowance to $1/8"$. To make opening for turning, cut a slit in organdy only (**Fig. 4**). Turn right side out and press to make **Unit 3**. Make 42 **Unit 3's**.

Fig. 4

Unit 3 (make 42)

7. Center 1 **Unit 3** on 1 **Unit 1**. Follow **Mock Hand Appliqué**, page 147, to stitch **Unit 3** to **Unit 1**. Working from wrong side and using care not to cut stitching or appliqué, use scissors to cut away background approximately $1/4"$ inside stitching line to make **Unit 4**. Repeat to make 42 **Unit 4's**.

Unit 4 (make 42)

8. To make triangle-square C's, place 1 navy and 1 white **rectangle C** right sides together. Referring to **Fig. 5**, follow **Making Triangle-Squares**, page 145, to make 30 **triangle-square C's**. Repeat with remaining **rectangle C's** to make a total of 180 **triangle-square C's**. (You will need 168 and have 12 left over.)

Fig. 5

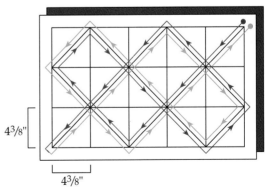

$4^3/8"$

$4^3/8"$

triangle-square C (make 180)

9. Place 1 **triangle-square C** and 1 organdy **small square** right sides together. Referring to **Fig. 6**, use **template B** to draw curved line on wrong side of organdy.

Fig. 6

10. Stitch on drawn line. Use pinking shears to trim seam allowance to ¹/₈" (**Fig. 7**). Turn right side out and press to make **Unit 5**. Make 168 **Unit 5's**.

Fig. 7   **Unit 5** (make 168)

11. Referring to **Block** diagram, follow **Mock Hand Appliqué**, page 147, to stitch 4 **Unit 5's** to corners of 1 **Unit 4** to make **Block**. Make 42 **Blocks**.

Block (make 42)

12. Sew 6 **Blocks** together to make row. Make 7 rows. Referring to **Quilt Top Diagram**, sew rows together to make center section of quilt top.
13. Follow **Adding Squared Borders**, page 148, to add **side**, then **top** and **bottom inner borders** to center section. Repeat to add **outer borders** to complete **Quilt Top**.

COMPLETING THE QUILT
1. Follow **Quilting**, page 149, to mark, layer, and quilt, using **Quilting Diagram** as a suggestion. Our quilt is hand quilted.
2. Cut a 30" square of binding fabric. Follow **Binding**, page 153, to bind quilt using 2¹/₂"w bias binding with mitered corners.

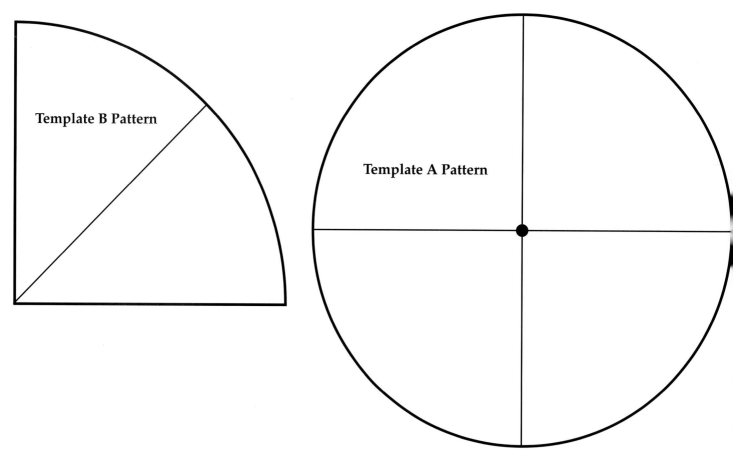

Template B Pattern

Template A Pattern

Quilt Top Diagram

Quilting Diagram

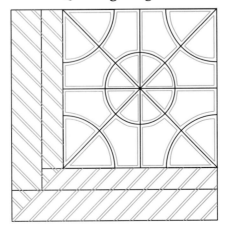

GOOD FORTUNE COLLECTION

The crisscrossing paths of the Good Fortune design depict the westward trails that America's pioneers followed, searching for their land of prosperity. A traditional pattern that's also known as Fly Foot and Devil's Puzzle, this simple design is really no devil at all to make! The solution to its ease is in rotary cutting — a technique that quickly yields the accurate triangles and rectangles needed for each square. The blocks are assembled using four pieced units, then joined side-by-side to create the intriguing arrangement. Completed with basic borders, this pattern is a fortunate find, indeed!

*S*imple floral motifs bloom on these creative cushions (below). For our welted pillow, a delightful decorative quilting pattern is encircled by a ring of the floral appliqués. A lovely appliquéd band completes the graceful gathers of our cinched pillow. The pretty posies also add a touch of cheer to the corners of our Good Fortune wall hanging (opposite). Print fabrics and stylized vines accentuate the blossoms, which are stitched in place following our invisible appliqué method.

123

GOOD FORTUNE QUILT

SKILL LEVEL: 1 2 3 4 5
BLOCK SIZE: 8" x 8"
QUILT SIZE: 74" x 82"

YARDAGE REQUIREMENTS
Yardage is based on 45"w fabric.

■ 4 yds of blue print
□ 3⁷/₈ yds of white solid
5 yds for backing
1 yd for binding
81" x 96" batting

CUTTING OUT THE PIECES
All measurements include a ¹/₄" seam allowance. Follow **Rotary Cutting**, *page 142, to cut fabric.*

1. **From blue print:** ■
   - Cut 2 lengthwise **side outer borders** 2⁵/₈" x 81".
   - Cut 2 lengthwise **top/bottom outer borders** 2⁵/₈" x 77".
   - From remaining fabric width, cut 18 strips 3⁵/₈"w. From these strips, cut 144 squares 3⁵/₈" x 3⁵/₈". Cut squares once diagonally to make 288 **large triangles**.
   - Cut 8 strips 4³/₈"w. From these strips, cut 144 **rectangles** 2¹/₄" x 4³/₈".
   - Cut 8 strips 2¹/₈"w. From these strips, cut 144 squares 2¹/₈" x 2¹/₈". Cut squares once diagonally to make 288 **small triangles**.

2. **From white solid:** □
   - Cut 2 lengthwise **side inner borders** 2³/₄" x 76".
   - Cut 2 lengthwise **top/bottom inner borders** 2³/₄" x 73".
   - From remaining fabric width, cut 18 strips 3⁵/₈"w. From these strips, cut 144 squares 3⁵/₈" x 3⁵/₈". Cut squares once diagonally to make 288 **large triangles**.
   - Cut 8 strips 4³/₈"w. From these strips, cut 144 **rectangles** 2¹/₄" x 4³/₈".
   - Cut 8 strips 2¹/₈"w. From these strips, cut 144 squares 2¹/₈" x 2¹/₈". Cut squares once diagonally to make 288 **small triangles**.

ASSEMBLING THE QUILT TOP
Follow **Piecing and Pressing**, *page 144, to make quilt top.*

1. Sew 2 blue **small triangles** and 1 white **rectangle** together to make **Unit 1a**. Make 144 **Unit 1a's**. Sew 2 white **small triangles** and 1 blue **rectangle** together to make **Unit 1b**. Make 144 **Unit 1b's**.

Unit 1a (make 144)   **Unit 1b** (make 144)

2. Sew 2 blue **large triangles** and 1 **Unit 1a** together to make **Unit 2a**. Make 144 **Unit 2a's**. Sew 2 white **large triangles** and 1 **Unit 1b** together to make **Unit 2b**. Make 144 **Unit 2b's**.

Unit 2a (make 144)   **Unit 2b** (make 144)

3. Sew 2 **Unit 2a's** and 2 **Unit 2b's** together to make **Block**. Make 72 **Blocks**.

Block (make 72)

4. Sew 8 **Blocks** together to make **Row**. Make 9 **Rows**.

Row (make 9)

5. Referring to **Quilt Top Diagram**, sew **Rows** together to make center section of quilt top.
6. Follow **Adding Squared Borders**, page 148, to add **side**, then **top** and **bottom inner borders** to center section. Repeat to add outer borders to complete **Quilt Top**.

COMPLETING THE QUILT
1. Follow **Quilting**, page 149, to mark, layer, and quilt, using **Quilting Diagram** as a suggestion. Our quilt is hand quilted.
2. Cut a 30" square of binding fabric. Follow **Binding**, page 153, to bind quilt using 2¹/₂"w bias binding with mitered corners.

Quilting Diagram

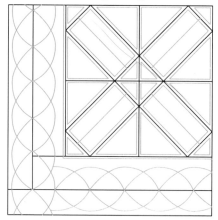

GOOD FORTUNE WALL HANGING

SKILL LEVEL: 1 2 3 4 5
BLOCK SIZE: 8" x 8"
WALL HANGING SIZE: 36" x 36"

YARDAGE REQUIREMENT
Yardage is based on 45"w fabric.

- ⬜ ⁷/₈ yd of white solid
- ⬛ ⁷/₈ yd of blue solid
- ⬛ ¹/₄ yd of blue print
- 🔲 scraps of assorted fabrics for appliqués
  1¹/₄ yds for backing and hanging sleeve
  ⁵/₈ yd for binding
  40" x 40" binding

CUTTING OUT THE PIECES
All measurements include a ¹/₄" seam allowance. Follow Rotary Cutting, page 142, to cut fabric.

1. **From white solid:** ⬜
   - Cut 2 strips 4³/₈"w. From these strips, cut 21 **rectangles** 2¹/₄" x 4³/₈".
   - Cut 2 strips 3⁵/₈"w. From these strips, cut 16 squares 3⁵/₈" x 3⁵/₈". Cut squares once diagonally to make 32 **large triangles**.
   - Cut 1 strip 2¹/₈"w. From this strip, cut 16 squares 2¹/₈" x 2¹/₈". Cut squares once diagonally to make 32 **small triangles**.
   - Cut 2 strips 4¹/₂"w. From these strips, cut 12 **squares** 4¹/₂" x 4¹/₂".

2. **From blue solid:** ⬛
   - Cut 2 **side outer borders** 2¹/₂" x 34¹/₂".
   - Cut 2 **top/bottom outer borders** 2¹/₂" x 30¹/₂".
   - Cut 1 strip 4³/₈"w. From this strip, cut 16 **rectangles** 2¹/₄" x 4³/₈".
   - Cut 2 strips 3⁵/₈"w. From these strips, cut 21 squares 3⁵/₈" x 3⁵/₈". Cut squares once diagonally to make 42 **large triangles**.
   - Cut 2 strips 2¹/₈"w. From these strips, cut 21 squares 2¹/₈" x 2¹/₈". Cut squares once diagonally to make 42 **small triangles**.

3. **From blue print:** ⬛
   - Cut 2 **side inner borders** 1¹/₂" x 30¹/₂".
   - Cut 2 **top/bottom inner borders** 1¹/₂" x 28¹/₂".

4. **From remaining fabrics and scraps:** 🔲
   - Referring to **Wall Hanging Top Diagram**, use patterns, page 129, and follow **Preparing Fusible Appliqués**, page 146 to make 12 **flower**, 12 **flower center**, and 4 **corner trim** appliqués.

ASSEMBLING THE WALL HANGING TOP
Follow Piecing and Pressing, page 144, to make wall hanging top.

1. Follow Steps 1 and 2 of **Assembling the Quilt Top**, page 124, to make 21 **Unit 2a's** and 16 **Unit 2b's**. (You will need 21 **Unit 1a's** and 16 **Unit 1b's**.)

2. Sew 4 **squares**, 2 **Unit 2a's**, and 1 **Unit 2b** together to make **Row A**. Make 2 **Row A's**. Sew 2 **squares**, 3 **Unit 2a's** and 2 **Unit 2b's** together to make **Row B**. Make 2 **Row B's**. Sew 4 **Unit 2a's** and 3 **Unit 2b's** together to make **Row C**. Make 2 **Row C's**. Sew 4 **Unit 2b's** and 3 **Unit 2a's** together to make 1 **Row D**.

Row A (make 2)

Row B (make 2)

Row C (make 2)

Row D (make 1)

3. Referring to **Wall Hanging Top Diagram**, sew **Rows** together to make center section of wall hanging top.

4. Follow **Adding Squared Borders**, page 148, to add **top**, **bottom**, and then **side inner borders** to center section of wall hanging top. Repeat to add **outer borders** to center section of wall hanging top.

5. Referring to **Wall Hanging Top Diagram**, follow **Invisible Appliqué**, page 146, to stitch appliqués to wall hanging to complete **Wall Hanging Top**.

COMPLETING THE WALL HANGING

1. Follow **Quilting**, page 149, to mark, layer and quilt wall hanging, using **Wall Hanging Quilting Diagram** as a suggestion. Our wall hanging is hand quilted.

2. Follow **Making a Hanging Sleeve**, page 155, to attach hanging sleeve to wall hanging.

3. Cut a 21" square of binding fabric. Follow **Binding**, page 153, to bind wall hanging using 2¹/₂"w bias binding with mitered corners.

Wall Hanging Top Diagram

Wall Hanging Quilting Diagram

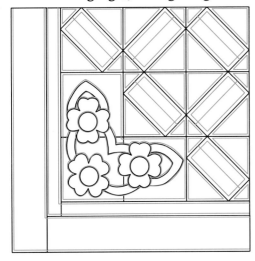

DOGWOOD PILLOW

PILLOW SIZE: 16" x 16"

SUPPLIES

16¹/₂" x 16¹/₂" white print fabric for pillow top
scraps of assorted fabrics for appliqués
20" x 20" pillow top backing fabric
16¹/₂" x 16¹/₂" pillow back fabric
20" x 20" batting
2 yds of 3"w bias fabric strip for welting (pieced
    as necessary)
2 yds of ³/₈" cord for welting
paper-backed fusible web
transparent monofilament thread
polyester fiberfill

MAKING THE PILLOW

1. Use patterns, page 129, and follow **Preparing Fusible Appliqués**, page 146, to make 12 **flower**, 12 **flower center**, and 4 **corner trim** appliqués.
2. Refer to **Dogwood Pillow Top Diagram** and follow **Invisible Appliqué**, page 146, to stitch appliqués to pillow top.
3. Follow **Quilting**, page 149, to mark, layer, and quilt pillow top, using **Dogwood Pillow Quilting Diagram** as a suggestion. Our pillow top is hand quilted.
4. Follow **Pillow Finishing**, page 155, to complete pillow with welting.

Dogwood Pillow Top Diagram

Dogwood Pillow Quilting Diagram

BANDED PILLOW

PILLOW SIZE: 9" x 18"

SUPPLIES

9¹/₂" x 18¹/₂" piece of white solid fabric for **pillow top backing**

27¹/₂" x 18¹/₂" piece of white solid fabric for **pillow top**

9¹/₂" x 18¹/₂" piece of blue print fabric for **pillow back**

4¹/₄" x 9¹/₂" piece of fabric for **band backing**

5" x 5" **square** each of white print and blue solid fabric for triangle-units

2¹/₄" x 4¹/₄" rectangle of white print fabric

assorted fabric scraps for appliqués

2 strips of fabric 2¹/₂" x 9¹/₂" for band binding

4¹/₄" x 9¹/₂" piece of batting

paper-backed fusible web

transparent monofilament thread

polyester fiberfill

MAKING THE PILLOW

All measurements include a ¹/₄" seam allowance. Follow Piecing and Pressing, page 144, to make pillow.

1. Place white print and blue solid **squares** right sides together. Referring to **Fig. 1a**, draw a diagonal line from corner to corner. Stitch ¹/₄" on both sides of drawn line; cut apart along drawn line (**Fig 1b**) to make 2 **triangle-squares**.

Fig. 1a   **Fig. 1b**

triangle-square (make 2)

2. Referring to **Fig. 2a**, place **triangle-squares** right sides and opposite colors together, matching seams. Referring to **Fig. 2b**, draw a diagonal line from corner to corner. Stitch ¹/₄" on both sides of drawn line. Cut apart on drawn line and press open to make 2 **triangle units** .

Fig. 2a   **Fig. 2b**

triangle unit (make 2)

3. Sew **triangle units** and **rectangle** together to make **pieced band**.

pieced band

4. Use patterns, page 129, and follow **Preparing Fusible Appliqués**, page 146, to make 3 **flower** and 3 **flower center** appliqués.

5. Refer to **Banded Pillow Top Diagram** and follow **Invisible Appliqué**, page 146, to stitch appliqués to **pieced band**.

6. Follow **Quilting**, page 149, to mark, layer, and quilt **pieced band**. Our pieced band is hand quilted in the ditch along seam lines and around appliqués.

7. Matching wrong sides and raw edges, press strips for band binding in half lengthwise.

8. Matching raw edges and using a ¹/₄" seam allowance, sew 1 length of binding to each long edge of **pieced band**. Fold binding over to band backing and pin pressed edges in place, covering stitching line; blindstitch binding to backing.

9. Baste ¹/₂" and ¹/₄" from long raw edges of pillow top. Pull basting threads, drawing up gathers to measure 9¹/₂".

10. Layer gathered pillow top and pillow top backing together. Stitch together along raw edges.

11. Center **pieced band** on top of gathered pillow top; pin in place.

12. With right sides facing and leaving an opening for turning, sew pillow top and pillow backing together. Turn right side out; stuff with fiberfill. Blindstitch opening closed.

Banded Pillow Top Diagram

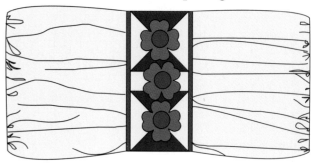

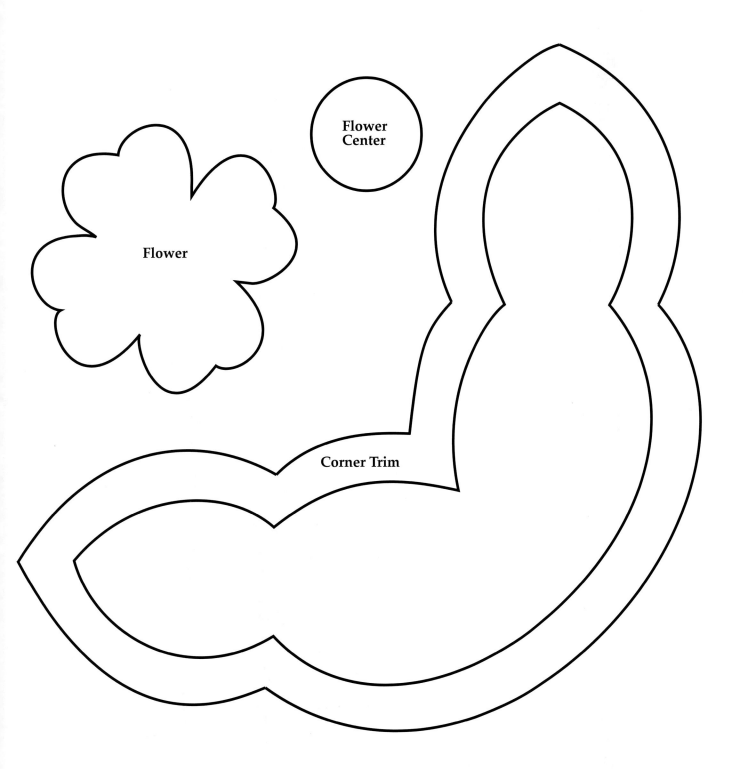

Flower Center

Flower

Corner Trim

OAK AND LAUREL COLLECTION

As a divided nation marched into the Civil War, quilters united their talents to support the troops. Splendid quilts created for auctions and raffles reflected the quilters' allegiance — Northern quilts sported eagles and other Union symbols, while Southern quilts incorporated symbolic floral appliqués. Our Oak and Laurel quilt typifies the Confederate style, representing the hope for perseverance and peace. The motifs are fused in place on each plain block, then machine appliquéd using clear nylon thread. For a pleasing finish, the pillow flip is accented with an elongated oak leaf design.

Four Oak and Laurel motifs are used for this pretty wall hanging (opposite). The sawtooth border is created with quick grid-pieced triangle-squares. We borrowed design elements from the wall hanging to create lovely throw pillows (below). A trio of laurel branches accents the ruffled pillow, and the roll pillow is enhanced with sawtooth edging and elegant bows.

OAK AND LAUREL QUILT

SKILL LEVEL: 1 2 3 **4** 5
BLOCK SIZE: 15" x 15"
QUILT SIZE: 83" x 108"

YARDAGE REQUIREMENTS

Yardage is based on 45"w fabric.

- 7¹/₂ yds of cream print
- 4 yds of blue print
- ³/₈ yd of dark blue print
  20 yds of navy ¹/₄"w double fold bias tape
  7³/₄ yds for backing
  1 yd for binding
  120" x 120" batting

You will also need:
  paper-backed fusible web
  transparent monofilament thread

CUTTING OUT THE PIECES

All measurements include a ¹/₄" seam allowance. Follow Rotary Cutting, page 142, to cut fabric.

1. **From cream print:**
   - Cut 2 lengthwise **side middle borders** 6¹/₂" x 108".
   - Cut 1 lengthwise **bottom middle border** 6¹/₂" x 68".
   - Cut 1 lengthwise **pillow flip** 23" x 62".
   - Cut 20 **large squares** 17" x 17".

2. **From blue print:**
   - Cut 2 lengthwise **side outer borders** 3¹/₂" x 111".
   - Cut 2 lengthwise **side inner borders** 2¹/₂" x 102".
   - Cut 1 lengthwise **bottom outer border** 3¹/₂" x 80".
   - Cut 1 lengthwise **bottom inner border** 2¹/₂" x 64".

PREPARING THE APPLIQUÉS

Use patterns, page 139, and follow Preparing Fusible Appliqués, page 146, to make appliqués.

1. **From blue print:**
   - Cut 88 **A's**.
   - Cut 336 **B's**.
   - Cut 176 **C's**.

2. **From dark blue print:**
   - Cut 80 **D's**.
   - Cut 26 **E's**.

3. **From navy bias tape:**
   - Cut 2 pieces 13"l for **short stems**.
   - Cut 40 pieces 16"l for **long stems**.

ASSEMBLING THE QUILT TOP

Follow Piecing and Pressing, page 144, to make quilt top.

1. Referring to **Block** diagram, follow **Invisible Appliqué**, page 146, to stitch **long stems** and **appliqués** to **large squares**. Trim squares to measure 15¹/₂" x 15¹/₂" to make a total of 20 **Blocks**.

Block (make 20)

2. Referring to **Pillow Flip Diagram**, follow **Invisible Appliqué**, page 146, to stitch **short stems** and **appliqués** to **pillow flip**. Trim **pillow flip** to measure 21¹/₂" x 60¹/₂".

Pillow Flip Diagram

3. Sew 4 **Blocks** together to make row. Make 5 rows.
4. Referring to **Quilt Top Diagram**, page 135, sew rows together to make center section of quilt top.
5. Sew **pillow flip** to top edge of center section.
6. Refer to **Adding Squared Borders**, page 148, to sew **bottom**, then **side inner borders** to center section. Repeat to add **middle** and **outer borders** to complete **Quilt Top**.

COMPLETING THE QUILT

1. Follow **Quilting**, page 149, to mark, layer, and quilt, using **Quilting Diagram**, page 136, as a suggestion. Our quilt is hand quilted.
2. Cut a 33" square of binding fabric. Follow **Binding**, page 153, to bind quilt using 2¹/₂"w bias binding with mitered corners.

OAK AND LAUREL WALL HANGING

SKILL LEVEL: 1 2 3 4 5
BLOCK SIZE: 15" x 15"
WALL HANGING SIZE: 35" x 35"

YARDAGE REQUIREMENTS

Yardage is based on 45"w fabric.

- 1³/₈ yds of cream print
- ¹/₂ yd of dark blue print
- ¹/₂ yd of blue print
  4 yds of navy ¹/₄"w double fold bias tape
  1¹/₄ yds for backing and hanging sleeve
  ⁵/₈ yd for binding
  38" x 38" batting

You will also need:
  paper-backed fusible web
  transparent monofilament thread

CUTTING OUT THE PIECES

All measurements include a ¹/₄" seam allowance. Follow Rotary Cutting, page 142, to cut fabric.

1. **From cream print:**
   - Cut 2 **rectangles** 10" x 16" for triangle-squares.
   - Cut 4 **large squares** 17" x 17".
   - Cut 4 **small squares** 2¹/₂" x 2¹/₂".

2. **From dark blue print:**
   - Cut 2 **rectangles** 10" x 16" for triangle-squares.

PREPARING THE APPLIQUÉS

*Use patterns, page 139, and follow **Preparing Fusible Appliqués**, page 146, to make appliqués.*

1. **From blue print:**
   - Cut 16 **A's**.
   - Cut 64 **B's**.
   - Cut 32 **C's**.

2. **From dark blue print:**
   - Cut 16 **D's**.
   - Cut 4 **E's**.

3. **From navy bias tape:**
   - Cut 8 pieces 16"l for **stems**.

ASSEMBLING THE WALL HANGING TOP

*Follow **Piecing and Pressing**, page 144, to make wall hanging top.*

1. Referring to **Block** diagram, page 134, follow **Invisible Appliqué**, page 146, to stitch **stems** and **appliqués** to **large squares**. Trim squares to measure 15¹/₂" x 15¹/₂" to make a total of 4 **Blocks**.

2. Referring to **Wall Hanging Top Diagram**, sew **Blocks** together to make center section of wall hanging top.

3. To make triangle-squares, place 1 cream and 1 dark blue **rectangle** right sides together. Referring to **Fig. 1**, follow **Making Triangle-Squares**, page 145, to make 30 **triangle-squares**. Repeat with remaining **rectangles** to make a total of 60 **triangle-squares**.

Fig. 1

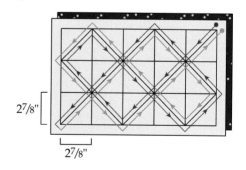

2⁷/₈"

2⁷/₈"

triangle-square (make 60)

4. Sew 15 **triangle-squares** together to make **Border**. Make 4 **Borders**.

Border (make 4)

5. Sew 1 **Border** to each side edge of center section. Sew 1 **small square** to each end of each remaining **Border**. Sew **Borders** to top and bottom edges of center section to complete **Wall Hanging Top**.

COMPLETING THE WALL HANGING

1. Follow **Quilting**, page 149, to mark, layer, and quilt wall hanging, using **Quilting Diagram** as a suggestion. Our wall hanging is hand quilted.
2. Follow **Making a Hanging Sleeve**, page 155, to attach hanging sleeve to wall hanging.
3. Cut a 20" square of binding fabric. Follow **Binding**, page 153, to bind wall hanging using 2¹/₂"w bias binding with mitered corners.

Quilting Diagram

Wall Hanging Top Diagram

137

APPLIQUÉ PILLOW

PILLOW SIZE: 18" x 18" (with ruffle)

SUPPLIES

- ☐ 13" x 13" square of cream print fabric for background
- ▨ scraps of blue and dark blue print fabrics for appliqués
  1 yd of navy ¼"w double fold bias tape
  17" x 17" pillow top backing fabric
  17" x 17" batting
  13" x 13" pillow back fabric
  1½ yds of 2"w bias fabric strip for welting
  1½ yds of 7/32" cord for welting
  7" x 96" fabric strip (pieced as necessary) for ruffle
  paper-backed fusible web
  transparent monofilament thread
  polyester fiberfill

MAKING THE PILLOW

Follow Piecing and Pressing, page 144, to make pillow.

1. Cut 2 pieces of bias tape 6"l and 1 piece 7½"l.
2. Use patterns, page 139, and follow **Preparing Fusible Appliqués**, page 146, to make 2 **B's**, 6 **C's**, and 3 **D's** from scraps.
3. Referring to **Pillow Top Diagram**, follow **Invisible Appliqué**, page 146, to stitch bias tape pieces and appliqués to background to complete pillow top.
4. Follow **Quilting**, page 149, to layer and quilt pillow top, using **Quilting Diagram** as a suggestion. Our pillow top is hand quilted.
5. Trim batting and backing even with edges of pillow top.
6. Follow **Pillow Finishing**, page 155, to complete pillow with welting and ruffle.

Pillow Top Diagram

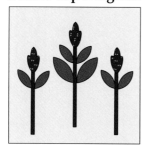

Quilting Diagram

ROLL PILLOW

YARDAGE REQUIREMENTS

Yardage is based on 45"w fabric.

- ☐ ½ yd of cream print
- ▨ ¼ yd of dark blue print
  1¾ yds of 2½"w navy grosgrain ribbon

You will also need:
  2 strong rubber bands
  polyester fiberfill

CUTTING OUT THE PIECES

Measurements include a ¼" seam allowance. Follow Rotary Cutting, page 142, to cut fabric.

1. **From cream print:** ☐
   - Cut 2 **end pieces** 15" x 20½".
   - Cut 1 **center piece** 7½" x 20½".
   - Cut 1 **rectangle** 7" x 16" for triangle-squares.

2. **From dark blue print:**
   - Cut 1 **rectangle** 7" x 16" for triangle-squares.

MAKING THE PILLOW

Follow Piecing and Pressing, page 144, to make pillow.

1. To make triangle-squares, place cream and dark blue **rectangles** right sides together. Referring to **Fig. 1**, follow **Making Triangle-Squares**, page 145, to make 20 **triangle-squares**.

Fig. 1

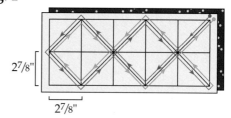

2⅞"
2⅞"

triangle-square (make 20)

2. Sew 10 **triangle-squares** together to make **Unit 1**. Sew 10 **triangle-squares** together to make **Unit 2**.

Unit 1 (make 1)

Unit 2 (make 1)

3. Referring to **Assembly Diagram**, sew **end pieces**, **Unit 1**, **Unit 2**, and **center piece** together. Sew long edges together to form a tube.
4. At each end of tube, press raw edge ½" to wrong side; press 5" to wrong side again and stitch in place. Turn right side out and press.
5. Wrap 1 rubber band around tube 5" from 1 end. Stuff tube with fiberfill and wrap remaining rubber band around tube 5" from remaining end.
6. Cut ribbon in half. Tie 1 ribbon length into a bow around each end of pillow, covering rubber bands; trim ribbon ends.

Assembly Diagram

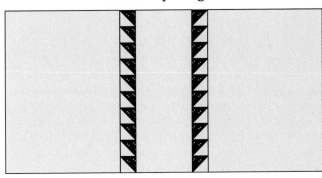

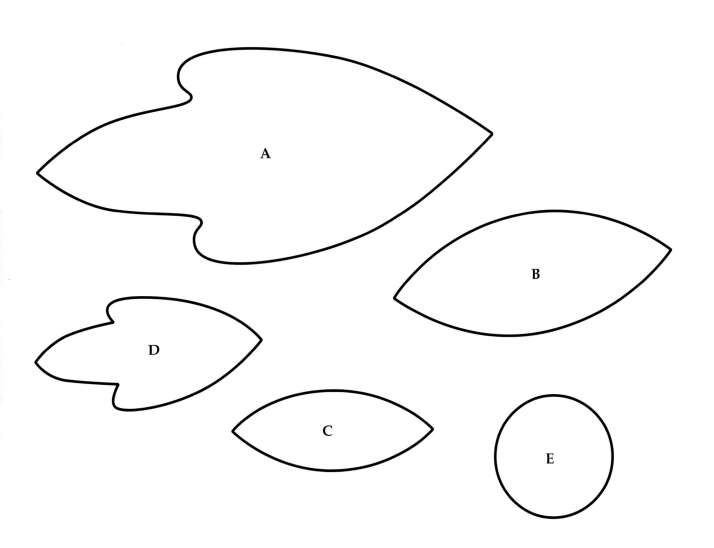

GENERAL INSTRUCTIONS

Complete instructions are given for making each of the quilts and other projects shown in this book. Skill levels indicated for quilts and wall hangings may help you choose the right project. To make your quilting easier and more enjoyable, we encourage you to carefully read all of the general instructions, study the color photographs, and familiarize yourself with the individual project instructions before beginning a project.

QUILTING SUPPLIES

This list includes the tools you need for basic quick-method quiltmaking, plus additional supplies used for special techniques. Unless otherwise specified, all items may be found in your favorite fabric store or quilt shop.

Batting — Batting is most commonly available in polyester, cotton, or a polyester/cotton blend (see **Choosing and Preparing the Batting**, page 151).

Cutting mat — A cutting mat is a special mat designed to be used with a rotary cutter. A mat that measures approximately 18" x 24" is a good size for most cutting.

Eraser — A soft white fabric eraser or white art eraser may be used to remove pencil marks from fabric. Do not use a colored eraser, as the dye may discolor fabric.

Iron — An iron with both steam and dry settings and a smooth, clean soleplate is necessary for proper pressing.

Marking tools — There are many different marking tools available (see **Marking Quilting Lines**, page 150). A silver quilter's pencil is a good marker for both light and dark fabrics.

Masking tape — Two widths of masking tape, 1"w and 1/4"w, are helpful when quilting. The 1"w tape is used to secure the backing fabric to a flat surface when layering the quilt. The 1/4"w tape may be used as a guide when outline quilting.

Needles — Two types of needles are used for hand sewing: *Betweens*, used for quilting, are short and strong for stitching through layered fabric and batting. *Sharps* are longer, thinner needles used for basting and other hand sewing. For *sewing machine needles*, we recommend size 10 to 14 or 70 to 90 universal (sharp-pointed) needles.

Paper-backed fusible web — This iron-on adhesive with paper backing is used to secure fabric cutouts to another fabric when appliquéing. If the cutouts will be stitched in place, purchase a lighter weight web that will not gum up your sewing machine needle. A heavier weight web is used for appliqués that are fused in place with no stitching.

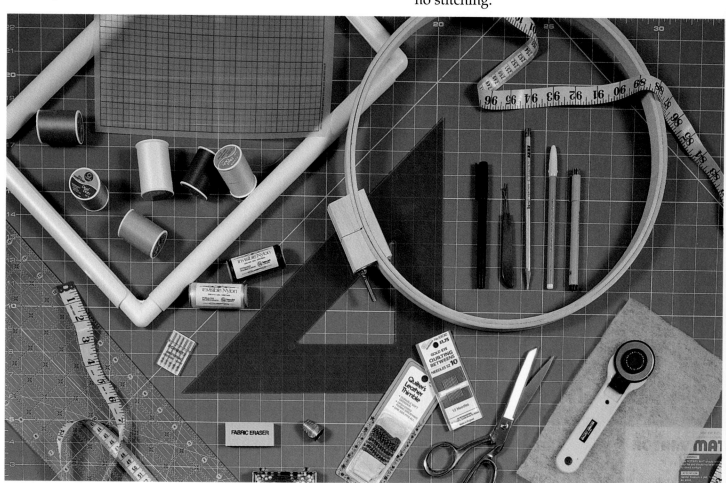

Permanent fine-point pen — A permanent pen is used to mark templates and stencils and to sign and date quilts. Test pen on fabric to make sure it will not bleed or wash out.

Pins — Straight pins made especially for quilting are extra long with large round heads. Glass head pins will stand up to occasional contact with a hot iron. Some quilters prefer extra-fine dressmaker's silk pins. If you are machine quilting, you will need a large supply of 1" long (size 01) rustproof safety pins for pin-basting.

Quilting hoop or frame — Quilting hoops and frames are designed to hold the 3 layers of a quilt together securely while you quilt. Many different types and sizes are available, including round and oval wooden hoops, frames made of rigid plastic pipe, and large floor frames made of either material. A 14" or 16" hoop allows you to quilt in your lap and makes your quilting portable.

Rotary cutter — The rotary cutter is the essential tool for quick-method quilting techniques. The cutter consists of a round, sharp blade mounted on a handle with a retractable blade guard for safety. It should be used only with a cutting mat and rotary cutting ruler. Two sizes are generally available; we recommend the larger (45 mm) size.

Rotary cutting ruler — A rotary cutting ruler is a thick, clear acrylic ruler made specifically for use with a rotary cutter. It should have accurate ⅛" crosswise and lengthwise markings and markings for 45° and 60° angles. A 6" x 24" ruler is a good size for most cutting. An additional 6" x 12" ruler or 12½" square ruler is helpful when cutting wider pieces. Many specialty rulers are available that make specific cutting tasks faster and easier.

Scissors — Although most fabric cutting will be done with a rotary cutter, sharp, high-quality scissors are still needed for some cutting. A separate pair of scissors for cutting paper and plastic is recommended. Smaller scissors are handy for clipping threads.

Seam ripper — A good seam ripper with a fine point is useful for removing stitching.

Sewing machine — A sewing machine that produces a good, even straight stitch is all that is necessary for most quilting. Zigzag stitch capability is necessary for **Invisible Appliqué**, page 146. Clean and oil your machine often and keep the tension set properly.

Stabilizer — Commercially made, non-woven material or paper stabilizer is placed behind background fabric when doing **Invisible Appliqué**, page 146, to provide a more stable stitching surface.

Tape measure — A flexible 120" long tape measure is helpful for measuring a quilt top before adding borders.

Template material — Sheets of translucent plastic, often pre-marked with a grid, are made especially for making templates and quilting stencils.

Thimble — A thimble is necessary when hand quilting. Thimbles are available in metal, plastic, or leather and in many sizes and styles. Choose a thimble that fits well and is comfortable.

Thread — Several types of thread are used for quiltmaking: *General-purpose* sewing thread is used for basting, piecing, and some appliquéing. Choose high-quality cotton or cotton-covered polyester thread in light and dark neutrals, such as ecru and grey, for your basic supplies. *Quilting* thread is stronger than general-purpose sewing thread, and some brands have a coating to make them slide more easily through the quilt layers. Some machine appliqué projects in this book use *transparent monofilament* (clear nylon) thread. Use a very fine (.004 mm) soft nylon thread that is not stiff or wiry. Choose clear nylon thread for white or light fabrics or smoke nylon thread for darker fabrics.

Triangle — A large plastic right-angle triangle (available in art and office supply stores) is useful in rotary cutting for making first cuts to "square up" raw edges of fabric and for checking to see that cuts remain at right angles to the fold.

Walking foot — A walking foot, or even-feed foot, is needed for straight-line machine quilting. This special foot will help all 3 layers move at the same rate over the feed dogs to provide a smoother quilted project.

FABRICS
SELECTING FABRICS

Choose high-quality, medium-weight 100% cotton fabrics such as broadcloth or calico. All-cotton fabrics hold a crease better, fray less, and are easier to quilt than cotton/polyester blends. All the fabrics for a quilt should be of comparable weight and weave. Check the end of the fabric bolt for fiber content and width.

The yardage requirements listed for each project are based on 45" wide fabric with a "usable" width of 42" after shrinkage and trimming selvages. Your actual usable width will probably vary slightly from fabric to fabric. Though most fabrics will yield 42" or more, if you find a fabric that you suspect will yield a narrower usable width, you will need to purchase additional yardage to compensate. Our recommended yardage lengths should be adequate for occasional resquaring of fabric when many cuts are required, but it never hurts to buy a little more fabric for insurance against a narrower usable width, the occasional cutting error, or to have on hand for making coordinating projects.

PREPARING FABRICS

All fabrics should be washed, dried, and pressed before cutting.

1. To check colorfastness before washing, cut a small piece of the fabric and place in a glass of hot water with a small amount of detergent. Leave fabric in the water for a few minutes. Remove fabric from water and blot with white paper towels. If any color bleeds onto the towels, wash the fabric separately with warm water and detergent, then rinse until the water runs clear. If fabric continues to bleed, choose another fabric.
2. Unfold yardage and separate fabrics by color. To help reduce raveling, use scissors to snip a small triangle from each corner of your fabric pieces. Machine wash fabrics in warm water with a small amount of mild laundry detergent. Do not use fabric softener. Rinse well and then dry fabrics in the dryer, checking long fabric lengths occasionally to make sure they are not tangling.
3. To make ironing easier, remove fabrics from dryer while they are slightly damp. Refold each fabric lengthwise (as it was on the bolt) with wrong sides together and matching selvages. If necessary, adjust slightly at selvages so that fold lays flat. Press each fabric using a steam iron set on "Cotton."

ROTARY CUTTING

*Based on the idea that you can easily cut strips of fabric and then cut those strips into smaller pieces, rotary cutting has brought speed and accuracy to quiltmaking. Observe safety precautions when using the rotary cutter, since it is extremely sharp. Develop a habit of retracting the blade guard **just before** making a cut and closing it **immediately afterward**, before laying down the cutter.*

1. Follow **Preparing Fabrics**, this page, to wash, dry, and press fabrics.
2. Cut all strips from the selvage-to-selvage width of the fabric unless otherwise indicated in project instructions. Place fabric on the cutting mat, as shown in **Fig. 1**, with the fold of the fabric toward you. To straighten the uneven fabric edge, make the first "squaring up" cut by placing the right edge of the rotary cutting ruler over the left raw edge of the fabric. Place right-angle triangle (or another rotary cutting ruler) with the lower edge carefully aligned with the fold and the left edge against the ruler (**Fig. 1**). Hold the ruler firmly with your left hand, placing your little finger off the left edge to anchor the ruler. Remove the triangle, pick up the rotary cutter, and retract the blade guard. Using a smooth downward motion, make the cut by running the blade of the rotary cutter firmly along the right edge of the ruler (**Fig. 2**). **Always** cut in a direction **away** from your body and **immediately** close the blade guard after each cut.

Fig. 1

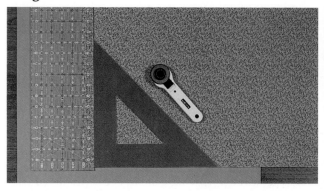

Fig. 2

3. To cut each of the strips required for a project, place the ruler over the cut edge of the fabric, aligning desired marking on the ruler with the cut edge (**Fig. 3**); make the cut. When cutting several strips from a single piece of fabric, it is important to occasionally use the ruler and triangle to ensure that cuts are still at a perfect right angle to the fold. If not, repeat Step 2 to straighten.

Fig. 3

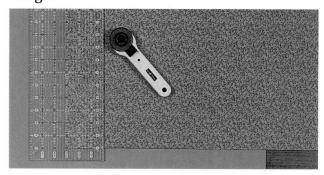

4. To square up selvage ends of a strip before cutting pieces, refer to **Fig. 4** and place folded strip on mat with selvage ends to your right. Aligning a horizontal marking on ruler with 1 long edge of strip, use rotary cutter to trim selvage to make end of strip square and even (**Fig. 4**). Turn strip (or entire mat) so that cut end is to your left before making subsequent cuts.

Fig. 4

5. Pieces such as rectangles and squares can now be cut from strips. (Cutting other shapes such as diamonds is discussed in individual project instructions.) Usually strips remain folded, and pieces are cut in pairs after ends of strips are squared up. To cut squares or rectangles from a strip, place ruler over left end of strip, aligning desired marking on ruler with cut end of strip. To ensure perfectly square cuts, align a horizontal marking on ruler with 1 long edge of strip (**Fig. 5**) before making the cut.

Fig. 5

6. To cut 2 triangles from a square, cut square the size indicated in the project instructions. Cut square once diagonally to make 2 triangles (**Fig. 6**).

Fig. 6

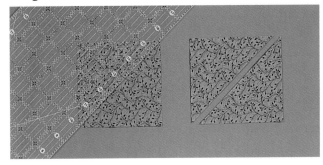

7. To cut 4 triangles from a square, cut square the size indicated in the project instructions. Cut square twice diagonally to make 4 triangles (**Fig. 7**). You may find it helpful to use a small rotary cutting mat so that the mat can be turned to make second cut without disturbing fabric pieces.

Fig. 7

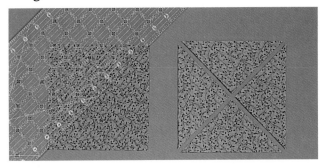

8. After some practice, you may want to try stacking up to 6 fabric layers when making cuts. When stacking strips, match long cut edges and follow Step 4 to square up ends of strip stack. Carefully turn stack (or entire mat) so that squared-up ends are to your left before making subsequent cuts. After cutting, check accuracy of pieces. Some shapes, such as diamonds, are more difficult to cut accurately in stacks.

9. In some cases, strips will be sewn together into strip sets before being cut into smaller units. When cutting a strip set, align a seam in strip set with a horizontal marking on the ruler to maintain square cuts (**Fig. 8**). We do not recommend stacking strip sets for rotary cutting.

Fig. 8

10. Most borders for quilts in this book are cut along the more stable lengthwise grain to minimize wavy edges caused by stretching. To remove selvages before cutting lengthwise strips, place fabric on mat with selvages to your left and squared-up end at bottom of mat. Placing ruler over selvage and using squared-up edge instead of fold, follow Step 2, page 142, to cut away selvages as you did raw edges (**Fig. 9**). After making a cut the length of the mat, move the next section of fabric to be cut onto the mat. Repeat until you have removed selvages from required length of fabric.

Fig. 9

11. After removing selvages, place ruler over left edge of fabric, aligning desired marking on ruler with cut edge of fabric. Make cuts as in Step 3. After each cut, move next section of fabric onto mat as in Step 10.

TEMPLATE CUTTING

Our full-sized piecing template patterns have 2 lines – a solid cutting line and a dashed line showing the 1/4" seam allowance. Patterns for appliqué templates do not include seam allowances.

1. To make a template from a pattern, use a permanent fine-point pen to carefully trace pattern onto template plastic, making sure to transfer all alignment and grain line markings. Cut out template along inner edge of drawn line. Check template against original pattern for accuracy.

2. To make a template from a one-quarter pattern, use a ruler to draw a line down the center of a sheet of template plastic. Turn plastic 90° and draw a line down the center, perpendicular to the first line. Match grey lines of pattern to intersection of lines on plastic. Trace pattern. Turn plastic and trace pattern in remaining corners. Cut out template as in Step 1.

3. To use a template, place template on wrong side of fabric (unless otherwise indicated in project instructions), aligning grain line on template with straight grain of fabric. Use a sharp fabric-marking pencil to draw around template. Transfer all alignment markings to fabric. Cut out fabric piece using scissors or rotary cutting equipment.

PIECING AND PRESSING

Precise cutting, followed by accurate piecing and careful pressing, will ensure that all the pieces of your quilt top fit together well.

PIECING

Set sewing machine stitch length for approximately 11 stitches per inch. Use a new, sharp needle suited for medium-weight woven fabric.

Use a neutral-colored general-purpose sewing thread (not quilting thread) in the needle and in the bobbin. Stitch first on a scrap of fabric to check upper and bobbin thread tension; make any adjustments necessary.

For good results, it is **essential** that you stitch with an **accurate 1/4" seam allowance**. On many sewing machines, the measurement from the needle to the outer edge of the presser foot is 1/4". If this is the case with your machine, the presser foot is your best guide. If not, measure 1/4" from the needle and mark throat plate with a piece of masking tape. Special presser feet that are exactly 1/4" wide are also available for most sewing machines.

When piecing, **always** place pieces **right sides together** and **match raw edges**; pin if necessary. (If using straight pins, remove the pins just before they reach the sewing machine needle.)

Chain Piecing

Chain piecing whenever possible will make your work go faster and will usually result in more accurate piecing. Stack the pieces you will be sewing beside your machine in the order you will need them and in a position that will allow you to easily pick them up. Pick up each pair of pieces, carefully place them together as they will be sewn, and feed them into the machine one after the other. Stop between each pair only long enough to pick up the next pair; don't cut thread between pairs (**Fig. 10**). After all pieces are sewn, cut threads, press, and go on to the next step, chain piecing when possible.

Fig. 10

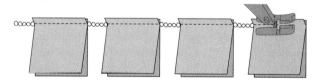

Sewing Across Seam Intersections

When sewing across the intersection of 2 seams, place pieces right sides together and match seams exactly, making sure seam allowances are pressed in opposite directions (**Fig. 11**). To prevent fabric from shifting, you may wish to pin in place.

Fig. 11

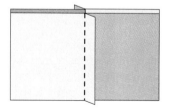

Sewing Bias Seams

Care should be used in handling and stitching bias edges since they stretch easily. After sewing the seam, carefully press seam allowance to 1 side, making sure not to stretch fabric.

Sewing Sharp Points

To ensure sharp points when joining triangular or diagonal pieces, stitch across the center of the "X" (shown in pink) formed on the wrong side by previous seams (**Fig. 12**).

Fig. 12

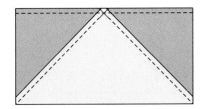

Making Triangle-Squares

The grid method for making triangle-squares is faster and more accurate than cutting and sewing individual triangles. Stitching before cutting the triangle-squares apart also prevents stretching the bias edges.

1. Follow project instructions to cut rectangles or squares of fabric for making triangle-squares. Place the indicated pieces right sides together and press.
2. On the wrong side of the lighter fabric, draw a grid of squares similar to that shown in **Fig. 13**. The size and number of squares are given in the project instructions.

Fig. 13

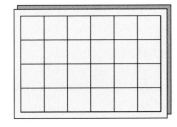

3. Following the example given in the project instructions, draw 1 diagonal line through each square in the grid (**Fig. 14**).

Fig. 14

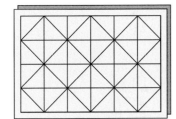

4. Stitch 1/4" on each side of all diagonal lines. For accuracy, it may be helpful to first draw your stitching lines onto the fabric, especially if your presser foot is not your 1/4" guide. In some cases, stitching may be done in a single continuous line. Project instructions include a diagram similar to **Fig. 15**, which shows stitching lines and the direction of the stitching.

Fig. 15

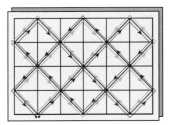

5. Use rotary cutter and ruler to cut along all drawn lines of the grid (**Fig. 16**). Each square of the grid will yield 2 triangle-squares.

Fig. 16

6. Carefully press triangle-squares open, pressing seam allowances toward darker fabric. Trim points of seam allowances that extend beyond edges of triangle-square (see **Fig. 21**).

Working with Diamonds and Set-in Seams

Piecing diamonds and sewing set-in seams require special handling. For best results, carefully follow the steps below.

1. When sewing 2 diamonds together, place pieces right sides together, carefully matching edges; pin. Mark a small dot 1/4" from corner of 1 piece as shown in **Fig. 17**. Stitch pieces together in the direction shown, stopping at center of dot and backstitching.

Fig. 17

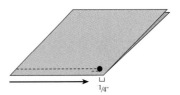

2. For best results, add side triangles, then corner squares to diamond sections. Mark corner of each piece to be set in with a small dot (**Fig. 18**).

Fig. 18

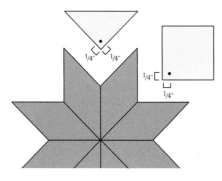

3. To sew first seam, match right sides and pin the triangle or square to the diamond on the left. Stitch seam from outer edge to the dot, backstitching at dot; clip threads (**Fig. 19**).

Fig. 19

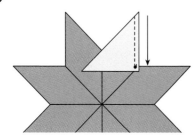

4. To sew the second seam, pivot the added triangle or square to match raw edges of next diamond. Beginning at dot, take 2 or 3 stitches, then backstitch, making sure not to backstitch into previous seam allowance. Continue stitching to outer edge (**Fig. 20**).

Fig. 20

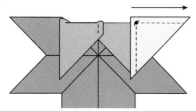

Trimming Seam Allowances

When sewing with diamond or triangle pieces, some seam allowances may extend beyond the edges of the sewn pieces. Trim away "dog ears" that extend beyond the edges of the sewn pieces (**Fig. 21**).

Fig. 21

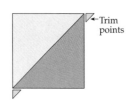

Trim points

PRESSING

Use a steam iron set on "Cotton" for all pressing. Press as you sew, taking care to prevent small folds along seamlines. Seam allowances are almost always pressed to one side, usually toward the darker fabric. However, to reduce bulk it may occasionally be necessary to press seam allowances toward the lighter fabric or even to press them open. In order to prevent a dark fabric seam allowance from showing through a light fabric, trim the darker seam allowance slightly narrower than the lighter seam allowance. To press long seams, such as those in long strip sets, without curving or other distortion, lay strips across the width of the ironing board.

APPLIQUÉ

PREPARING FUSIBLE APPLIQUÉS

Patterns are printed in reverse to enable you to use our speedy method of preparing appliqués. White or light-colored fabrics may need to be lined with fusible interfacing before applying fusible web to prevent darker fabrics from showing through.

1. Place paper-backed fusible web, web side down, over appliqué pattern. Use a pencil to trace pattern onto paper side of web as many times as indicated in project instructions for a single fabric. Repeat for additional patterns and fabrics.
2. Follow manufacturer's instructions to fuse traced patterns to wrong side of fabrics. Do not remove paper backing. (*Note:* Some pieces may be given as measurements, such as a 2" x 4" rectangle, instead of drawn patterns. Fuse web to wrong side of the fabrics indicated for these pieces.)
3. Use scissors to cut out appliqué pieces along traced lines; use rotary cutting equipment to cut out appliqué pieces given as measurements. Remove paper backing from all pieces.

INVISIBLE APPLIQUÉ

This machine appliqué method uses clear nylon thread to secure the appliqué pieces. Transparent monofilament (clear nylon) thread is available in 2 colors: clear and smoke. Use clear on white or very light fabrics and smoke on darker colors.

1. Referring to diagram and/or photo, arrange prepared appliqués on the background fabric and follow manufacturer's instructions to fuse in place.
2. Pin a stabilizer, such as paper or any of the commercially available products, on wrong side of background fabric before stitching appliqués in place.
3. Thread sewing machine with transparent monofilament thread; use general-purpose thread that matches background fabric in bobbin.
4. Set sewing machine for a very narrow width (approximately 1/16") zigzag stitch and a short

stitch length. You may find that loosening the top tension slightly will yield a smoother stitch.

5. Begin by stitching 2 or 3 stitches in place (drop feed dogs or set stitch length at 0) to anchor thread. Most of the zigzag stitch should be done on the appliqué with the right edges of the stitch falling at the very outside edge of the appliqué. Stitch over all exposed raw edges of appliqué pieces.

6. (Note: Dots on **Figs. 22 - 27** indicate where to leave needle in fabric when pivoting.) For **outside corners**, stitch just past the corner, stopping with the needle in **background** fabric (**Fig. 22**). Raise presser foot. Pivot project, lower presser foot, and stitch adjacent side (**Fig. 23**).

Fig. 22

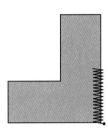

Fig. 23

7. For **inside corners**, stitch just past the corner, stopping with the needle in **appliqué** fabric (**Fig. 24**). Raise presser foot. Pivot project, lower presser foot, and stitch adjacent side (**Fig. 25**).

Fig. 24

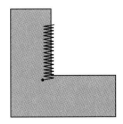

Fig. 25

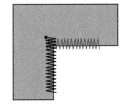

8. When stitching **outside** curves, stop with needle in **background** fabric. Raise presser foot and pivot project as needed. Lower presser foot and continue stitching, pivoting as often as necessary to follow curve (**Fig. 26**).

Fig. 26

9. When stitching **inside** curves, stop with needle in **appliqué** fabric. Raise presser foot and pivot project as needed. Lower presser foot and continue stitching, pivoting as often as necessary to follow curve (**Fig. 27**).

Fig. 27

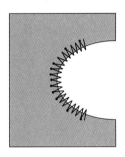

10. Do not backstitch at end of stitching. Pull threads to wrong side of background fabric; knot thread and trim ends.
11. Carefully tear away stabilizer.

MOCK HAND APPLIQUÉ

This technique uses the blindstitch on your sewing machine to achieve a look that closely resembles traditional hand appliqué. Using an updated method, appliqués are prepared with turned-under edges and then machine stitched to the background fabric. For best appliqué results, your sewing machine must have blindstitch capability with a variable stitch width. If your blindstitch width cannot be adjusted, you may still wish to try this technique to see if you are happy with the results. Some sewing machines have a narrower blindstitch width than others.

1. Follow project instructions to prepare appliqué pieces.
2. Thread needle of sewing machine with transparent monofilament thread; use general-purpose thread in bobbin in a color to match background fabric.
3. Set sewing machine for narrow blindstitch (just wide enough to catch 2 or 3 threads of the appliqué) and a very short stitch length (20 - 30 stitches per inch).
4. Arrange appliqué pieces on background fabric as described in project instructions. Use pins or hand baste to secure.

147

5. (*Note:* Follow Steps 6 - 9 of **Invisible Appliqué**, page 146, for needle position when pivoting.) Sew around edges of each appliqué so that the straight stitches fall on the background fabric very near the appliqué and the "hem" stitches barely catch the folded edge of the appliqué (**Fig. 28**).

Fig. 28

6. It is not necessary to backstitch at the beginning or end of stitching. End stitching by sewing ¹/₄" over the first stitches. Trim thread ends close to fabric.
7. To reduce bulk, turn project over and use scissors to cut away background fabric approximately ¹/₄" inside stitching line of appliqué as shown in **Fig. 29**.

Fig. 29

SATIN STITCH APPLIQUÉ

A good satin stitch is a smooth, almost solid line of zigzag stitching that covers the raw edges of appliqué pieces. Designs with layered appliqué pieces should be stitched beginning with the bottom pieces and ending with the pieces on top.

1. Follow Steps 1 and 2 of **Invisible Appliqué**, page 146.
2. Thread needle of sewing machine with general purpose thread that coordinates or contrasts with appliqué fabric and use thread that matches background fabric in the bobbin. Set sewing machine for a medium width (approximately ¹/₈") zigzag stitch and a very short stitch length and refer to Steps 3 - 11 of **Invisible Appliqué** to stitch appliqués in place.

BORDERS

Borders cut along the lengthwise grain will lie flatter than borders cut along the crosswise grain. In most cases, our instructions for cutting borders for bed-size quilts include an extra 2" of length at each end for "insurance"; borders will be trimmed after measuring completed center section of quilt top.

ADDING SQUARED BORDERS

1. Mark the center of each edge of quilt top.
2. Squared borders are usually added to top and bottom, then side edges of the center section of a quilt top. To add top and bottom borders, measure across center of quilt top to determine length of borders (**Fig. 30**). Trim top and bottom borders to the determined length.

Fig. 30

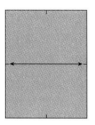

3. Mark center of 1 long edge of top border. Matching center marks and raw edges, pin border to quilt top, easing in any fullness; stitch. Repeat for bottom border.
4. Measure center of quilt top, including attached borders, to determine length of side borders. Trim side borders to the determined length. Repeat Step 3 to add borders to quilt top (**Fig. 31**).

Fig. 31

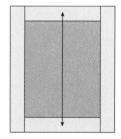

ADDING MITERED BORDERS

1. Mark the center of each edge of quilt top.
2. Mark center of 1 long edge of top border. Measure across center of quilt top (see **Fig. 30**). Matching center marks and raw edges, pin border to center of quilt top edge. Beginning at center of border, measure ¹/₂ the width of the quilt top in both directions and mark. Match marks on border with corners of quilt top and pin. Easing in any fullness, pin border to quilt top between center and corners. Sew border to

quilt top, beginning and ending seams **exactly** 1/4" from each corner of quilt top and backstitching at beginning and end of stitching (**Fig. 32**).

Fig. 32

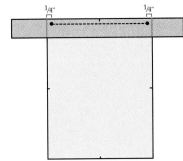

3. Repeat Step 2 to sew bottom, then side borders, to center section of quilt top. To temporarily move first 2 borders out of the way, fold and pin ends as shown in **Fig. 33**.

Fig. 33

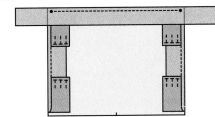

4. Fold 1 corner of quilt top diagonally with right sides together and matching edges. Use ruler to mark stitching line as shown in **Fig. 34**. Pin borders together along drawn line. Sew on drawn line, backstitching at beginning and end of stitching (**Fig. 35**).

Fig. 34

Fig. 35

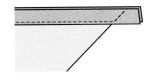

5. Turn mitered corner right side up. Check to make sure corner will lie flat with no gaps or puckers.
6. Trim seam allowance to 1/4"; press to 1 side.
7. Repeat Steps 4 - 6 to miter each remaining corner.

QUILTING

*Quilting holds the 3 layers (top, batting, and backing) of the quilt together and can be done by hand or machine. Our project instructions tell you which method is used on each project and show you quilting diagrams that can be used as suggestions for marking quilting designs. Because marking, layering, and quilting are interrelated and may be done in different orders depending on circumstances, please read the entire **Quilting** section, pages 149 - 152, before beginning the quilting process on your project.*

TYPES OF QUILTING

In the Ditch
Quilting very close to a seamline (**Fig. 36**) or appliqué (**Fig. 37**) is called "in the ditch" quilting. This type of quilting does not need to be marked and is indicated on our quilting diagrams with blue lines close to seamlines. When quilting in the ditch, quilt on the side **opposite** the seam allowance.

Fig. 36

Fig. 37

Outline Quilting
Quilting approximately 1/4" from a seam or appliqué is called "outline" quilting (**Fig. 38**). This type of quilting is indicated on our quilting diagrams by blue lines a short distance from seamlines. Outline quilting may be marked, or you may place 1/4"w masking tape along seamlines and quilt along the opposite edge of the tape. (Do not leave tape on quilt longer than necessary, since it may leave an adhesive residue.)

Fig. 38

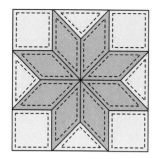

Ornamental Quilting

Quilting decorative lines or designs is called "ornamental" quilting (**Fig. 39**). Ornamental quilting is indicated on our quilting diagrams by blue lines. This type of quilting should be marked before you baste quilt layers together.

Fig. 39

MARKING QUILTING LINES

Fabric marking pencils, various types of chalk markers, and fabric marking pens with inks that disappear with exposure to air or water are readily available and work well for different applications. Lead pencils work well on light-color fabrics, but marks may be difficult to remove. White pencils work well on dark-color fabrics, and silver pencils show up well on many colors. Since chalk rubs off easily, it's a good choice if you are marking as you quilt. Fabric marking pens make more durable and visible markings, but the marks should be carefully removed according to manufacturer's instructions. Press down only as hard as necessary to make a visible line.

When you choose to mark your quilt, whether before or after the layers are basted together, is also a factor in deciding which marking tool to use. If you mark with chalk or a chalk pencil, handling the quilt during basting may rub off the markings. Intricate or ornamental designs may not be practical to mark as you quilt; mark these designs before basting using a more durable marker.

To choose marking tools, take all these factors into consideration and **test** different markers **on scrap fabric** until you find the one that gives the desired result.

USING QUILTING STENCILS

A wide variety of precut quilting stencils, as well as entire books of quilting patterns, are available. Using a stencil makes it easier to mark intricate or repetitive designs on your quilt top.

1. To make a stencil from a pattern, center template plastic over pattern and use a permanent marker to trace pattern onto plastic.
2. Use a craft knife with a single or double blade to cut narrow slits along traced lines (**Fig. 40**).

Fig. 40

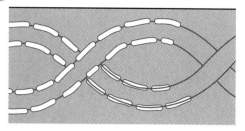

3. Use desired marking tool and stencil to mark quilting lines.

CHOOSING AND PREPARING THE BACKING

To allow for slight shifting of the quilt top during quilting, the backing should be approximately 4" larger on all sides for a bed-size quilt top or approximately 2" larger on all sides for a wall hanging. Yardage requirements listed for quilt backings are calculated for 45"w fabric. If you are making a bed-size quilt, using 90"w or 108"w fabric for the backing may eliminate piecing. To piece a backing using 45"w fabric, use the following instructions.

1. Measure length and width of quilt top; add 8" (4" for a wall hanging) to each measurement.
2. If quilt top is 76"w or less, cut backing fabric into 2 lengths slightly longer than the determined **length** measurement. Trim selvages. Place lengths with right sides facing and sew long edges together, forming a tube (**Fig. 41**). Match seams and press along 1 fold (**Fig. 42**). Cut along pressed fold to form a single piece (**Fig. 43**).

Fig. 41

Fig. 42

Fig. 43

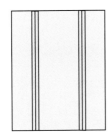

3. If quilt top is more than 76"w, cut backing fabric into 3 lengths slightly longer than the determined **width** measurement. Trim selvages. Sew long edges together to form a single piece.
4. Trim backing to correct size, if necessary, and press seam allowances open.

CHOOSING AND PREPARING THE BATTING

Choosing the right batting will make your quilting job easier. For fine hand quilting, choose a low-loft batting in any of the fiber types described here. Machine quilters will want to choose a low-loft batting that is all cotton or a cotton/polyester blend because the cotton helps "grip" the layers of the quilt. If the quilt is to be tied, a high-loft batting, sometimes called extra-loft or fat batting, is a good choice.

Batting is available in many different fibers. Bonded polyester batting is one of the most popular batting types. It is treated with a protective coating to stabilize the fibers and to reduce "bearding," a process in which batting fibers work their way out through the quilt fabrics. Other batting options include cotton/polyester batting, which combines the best of both polyester and cotton battings; all-cotton batting, which must be quilted more closely than polyester batting; and wool and silk battings, which are generally more expensive and usually only dry-cleanable.

Whichever batting you choose, read the manufacturer's instructions closely for any special notes on care or preparation. When you're ready to use your chosen batting in a project, cut batting the same size as the prepared backing.

LAYERING THE QUILT

1. Examine wrong side of quilt top closely; trim any seam allowances and clip any threads that may show through the front of the quilt. Press quilt top.
2. If quilt top is to be marked before layering, mark quilting lines (see **Marking Quilting Lines**, page 150).
3. Place backing **wrong** side up on a flat surface. Use masking tape to tape edges of backing to surface. Place batting on top of backing fabric. Smooth batting gently, being careful not to stretch or tear. Center quilt top **right** side up on batting.
4. If hand quilting, begin in the center and work toward the outer edges to hand baste all layers together. Use long stitches and place basting lines approximately 4" apart (**Fig. 44**). Smooth fullness or wrinkles toward outer edges.

Fig. 44

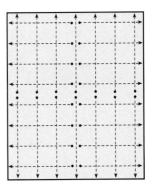

5. If machine quilting, use 1" rustproof safety pins to "pin-baste" all layers together, spacing pins approximately 4" apart. Begin at the center and work toward the outer edges to secure all layers. If possible, place pins away from areas that will be quilted, although pins may be removed as needed when quilting.

HAND QUILTING

The quilting stitch is a basic running stitch that forms a broken line on the quilt top and backing. Stitches on the quilt top and backing should be straight and equal in length.

1. Secure center of quilt in hoop or frame. Check quilt top and backing to make sure they are smooth. To help prevent puckers, always begin quilting in the center of the quilt and work toward the outside edges.
2. Thread needle with an 18" - 20" length of quilting thread; knot 1 end. Using a thimble, insert needle into quilt top and batting approximately 1/2" from where you wish to begin quilting. Bring needle up at the point where you wish to begin (**Fig. 45**); when knot catches on quilt top, give thread a quick, short pull to "pop" knot through fabric into batting (**Fig. 46**).

151

Fig. 45

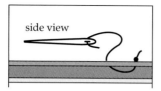

Fig. 46

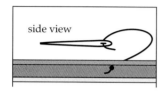

3. Holding the needle with your sewing hand and placing your other hand underneath the quilt, use thimble to push the tip of the needle down through all layers. As soon as needle touches your finger underneath, use that finger to push the tip of the needle only back up through the layers to top of quilt. (The amount of the needle showing above the fabric determines the length of the quilting stitch.) Referring to **Fig. 47**, rock the needle up and down, taking 3 - 6 stitches before bringing the needle and thread completely through the layers. Check the back of the quilt to make sure stitches are going through all layers. When quilting through a seam allowance or quilting a curve or corner, you may need to make 1 stitch at a time.

Fig. 47

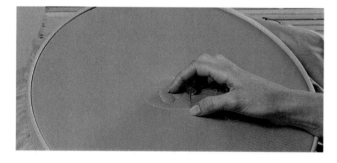

4. When you reach the end of your thread, knot thread close to the fabric and "pop" knot into batting; clip thread close to fabric.
5. Stop and move your hoop as often as necessary. You do not have to tie a knot every time you move your hoop; you may leave the thread dangling and pick it up again when you return to that part of the quilt.

MACHINE QUILTING

The following instructions are for straight-line quilting, which requires a walking foot or even-feed foot. The term "straight-line" is somewhat deceptive, since curves (especially gentle ones) as well as straight lines can be stitched with this technique.

152

1. Wind your sewing machine bobbin with general-purpose thread that matches the quilt backing. Do not use quilting thread. Thread the needle of your machine with transparent monofilament thread if you want your quilting to blend with your quilt top fabrics. Use decorative thread, such as a metallic or contrasting-color general-purpose thread, when you want the quilting lines to stand out more. Set the stitch length for 6 - 10 stitches per inch and attach the walking foot to sewing machine.
2. After pin-basting, decide which section of the quilt will have the longest continuous quilting line, oftentimes the area from center top to center bottom. Leaving the area exposed where you will place your first line of quilting, roll up each edge of the quilt to help reduce the bulk, keeping fabrics smooth. Smaller projects may not need to be rolled.
3. Start stitching at beginning of longest quilting line, using very short stitches for the first 1/4" to "lock" beginning of quilting line. Stitch across project, using one hand on each side of the walking foot to slightly spread the fabric and to guide the fabric through the machine. Lock stitches at end of quilting line.
4. Continue machine quilting, stitching longer quilting lines first to stabilize the quilt before moving on to other areas.

BINDING

Binding encloses the raw edges of your quilt. Because of its stretchiness, bias binding works well for binding projects with curves or rounded corners and tends to lie smooth and flat in any given circumstance. It is also more durable than other types of binding. Binding may also be cut from the straight lengthwise or crosswise grain of the fabric. You will find that straight-grain binding works well for projects with straight edges.

MAKING CONTINUOUS BIAS STRIP BINDING

Bias strips for binding can simply be cut and pieced to the desired length. However, when a long length of binding is needed, the "continuous" method is quick and accurate.

1. Cut a square from binding fabric the size indicated in the project instructions. Cut square in half diagonally to make 2 triangles.
2. With right sides together and using a 1/4" seam allowance, sew triangles together (**Fig. 48**); press seam allowance open.

Fig. 48

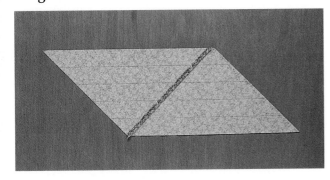

3. On wrong side of fabric, draw lines the width of the binding as specified in the project instructions, usually 2 1/2" (**Fig. 49**). Cut off any remaining fabric less than this width.

Fig. 49

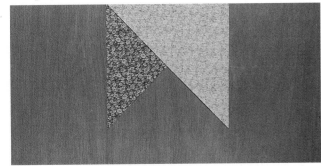

4. With right sides inside, bring short edges together to form a tube; match raw edges so that first drawn line of top section meets second drawn line of bottom section (**Fig. 50**).

Fig. 50

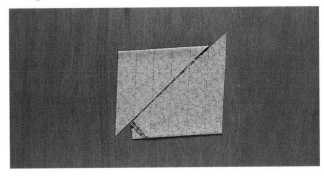

5. Carefully pin edges together by inserting pins through drawn lines at the point where drawn lines intersect, making sure the pins go through intersections on both sides. Using a 1/4" seam allowance, sew edges together. Press seam allowance open.
6. To cut continuous strip, begin cutting along first drawn line (**Fig. 51**). Continue cutting along drawn line around tube.

Fig. 51

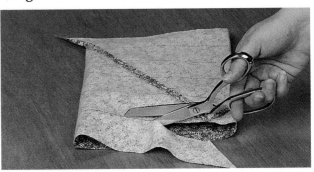

7. Trim ends of bias strip square.
8. Matching wrong sides and raw edges, press bias strip in half lengthwise to complete binding.

MAKING STRAIGHT-GRAIN BINDING

1. To determine length of strip needed if attaching binding with mitered corners, measure edges of the quilt and add 12".
2. To determine lengths of strips needed if attaching binding with overlapped corners, measure each edge of quilt; add 3" to each measurement.
3. Cut lengthwise or crosswise strips of binding fabric the determined length and the width called for in the project instructions. Strips may be pieced to achieve the necessary length.
4. Matching wrong sides and raw edges, press strip(s) in half lengthwise to complete binding.

ATTACHING BINDING WITH MITERED CORNERS

1. Press 1 end of binding diagonally (**Fig. 52**).

Fig. 52

2. Beginning with pressed end several inches from a corner, lay binding around quilt to make sure that seams in binding will not end up at a corner. Adjust placement if necessary. Matching raw edges of binding to raw edge of quilt top, pin binding to right side of quilt along 1 edge.
3. When you reach the first corner, mark ¼" from corner of quilt top (**Fig. 53**).

Fig. 53

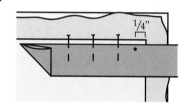

4. Using a ¼" seam allowance, sew binding to quilt, backstitching at beginning of stitching and when you reach the mark (**Fig. 54**). Lift needle out of fabric and clip thread.

Fig. 54

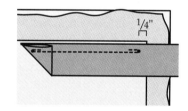

5. Fold binding as shown in **Figs. 55** and **56** and pin binding to adjacent side, matching raw edges. When you reach the next corner, mark ¼" from edge of quilt top.

Fig. 55

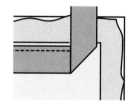

Fig. 56

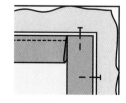

6. Backstitching at edge of quilt top, sew pinned binding to quilt (**Fig. 57**); backstitch when you reach the next mark. Lift needle out of fabric and clip thread.

Fig. 57

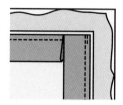

7. Repeat Steps 5 and 6 to continue sewing binding to quilt until binding overlaps beginning end by approximately 2". Trim excess binding.
8. If using 2½"w binding (finished size ½"), trim backing and batting a scant ¼" larger than quilt top so that batting and backing will fill the binding when it is folded over to the quilt backing. If using narrower binding, trim backing and batting even with edges of quilt top.
9. On 1 edge of quilt, fold binding over to quilt backing and pin pressed edge in place, covering stitching line (**Fig. 58**). On adjacent side, fold binding over, forming a mitered corner (**Fig. 59**). Repeat to pin remainder of binding in place.

Fig. 58   **Fig. 59**

10. Blindstitch binding to backing, taking care not to stitch through to front of quilt.

ATTACHING BINDING WITH OVERLAPPED CORNERS

1. Matching raw edges and using a ¼" seam allowance, sew a length of binding to top and bottom edges on right side of quilt.
2. If using 2½"w binding (finished size ½"), trim backing and batting from top and bottom edges a scant ¼" larger than quilt top so that batting and backing will fill the binding when it is folded over to the quilt backing. If using narrower binding, trim backing and batting even with edges of quilt top.
3. Trim ends of top and bottom binding even with edges of quilt top. Fold binding over to quilt backing and pin pressed edges in place, covering stitching line (**Fig. 60**); blindstitch binding to backing.

Fig. 60

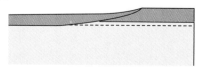

4. Leaving approximately 1½" of binding at each end, stitch a length of binding to each side edge of quilt. Trim backing and batting as in Step 2.
5. Trim each end of binding ½" longer than bound edge. Fold each end of binding over to quilt backing (**Fig. 61**); pin in place. Fold binding over to quilt backing and blindstitch in place, taking care not to stitch through to front of quilt.

Fig. 61

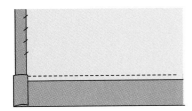

MAKING A HANGING SLEEVE

Attaching a hanging sleeve to the back of your wall hanging or quilt before the binding is added allows you to display your completed project on a wall.

1. Measure the width of the wall hanging top and subtract 1". Cut a piece of fabric 7"w by the determined measurement.
2. Press short edges of fabric piece ¼" to wrong side; press edges ¼" to wrong side again and machine stitch in place.
3. Matching wrong sides, fold piece in half lengthwise to form a tube.
4. Follow project instructions to sew binding to quilt top and to trim backing and batting. Before blindstitching binding to backing, match raw edges and stitch hanging sleeve to center top edge on back of wall hanging.
5. Finish binding wall hanging, treating the hanging sleeve as part of the backing.
6. Blindstitch bottom of hanging sleeve to backing, taking care not to stitch through to front of quilt.
7. Insert dowel or slat into hanging sleeve.

SIGNING AND DATING YOUR QUILT

Your completed quilt is a work of art and should be signed and dated. There are many different ways to do this, and you should pick a method that reflects the style of the quilt, the occasion for which it was made, and your own particular talents.

The following suggestions may give you an idea for recording the history of your quilt for future generations.

• Embroider your name, the date, and any additional information on the quilt top or

backing. You may choose embroidery floss colors that closely match the fabric you are working on, such as white floss on a white border, or contrasting colors may be used.
• Make a label from muslin and use a permanent marker to write your information. Your label may be as plain or as fancy as you wish. Stitch the label to the back of the quilt.
• Chart a cross-stitch label design that includes the information you wish and stitch it in colors that complement the quilt. Stitch the finished label to the quilt backing.

PILLOW FINISHING

Any quilt block may be made into a pillow. If desired, you may add welting and/or a ruffle to the pillow top before sewing the pillow top and back together.

ADDING WELTING TO PILLOW TOP

1. To make welting, use bias strip indicated in project instructions. (Or measure edges of pillow top and add 4". Measure circumference of cord and add 2". Cut a bias strip of fabric the determined measurement, piecing if necessary.)
2. Lay cord along center of bias strip on wrong side of fabric; fold strip over cord. Using a zipper foot, machine baste along length of strip close to cord. Trim seam allowance to the width you will use to sew pillow top and back together (see Step 2 of **Making the Pillow**, page 156).
3. Matching raw edges and beginning and ending 3" from ends of welting, baste welting to right side of pillow top. To make turning corners easier, clip seam allowance of welting at pillow top corners.
4. Remove approximately 3" of seam at 1 end of welting; fold fabric away from cord. Trim remaining end of welting so that cord ends meet exactly (**Fig. 62**).

Fig. 62

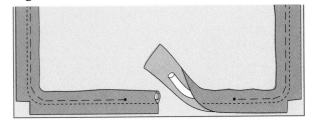

5. Fold short edge of welting fabric ½" to wrong side; fold fabric back over area where ends meet (**Fig. 63**).

Fig. 63

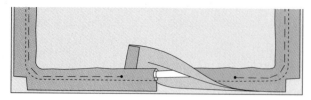

6. Baste remainder of welting to pillow top close to cord (**Fig. 64**).

Fig. 64

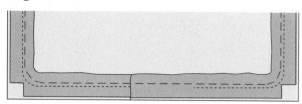

7. Follow **Making the Pillow** to complete pillow.

ADDING RUFFLE TO PILLOW TOP

1. To make ruffle, use fabric strip indicated in project instructions.
2. Matching right sides, use a ¼" seam allowance to sew short edges of ruffle together to form a large circle; press seam allowance open. To form ruffle, fold along length with wrong sides together and raw edges matching; press.
3. To gather ruffle, place quilting thread ¼" from raw edge of ruffle. Using a medium width zigzag stitch with medium stitch length, stitch over quilting thread, being careful not to catch quilting thread in stitching. Pull quilting thread, drawing up gathers to fit pillow top.
4. Matching raw edges, baste ruffle to right side of pillow top.
5. Follow **Making the Pillow** to complete pillow.

MAKING THE PILLOW

1. For pillow back, cut a piece of fabric the same size as pieced and quilted pillow top.
2. Place pillow back and pillow top right sides together. The seam allowance width you use will depend on the construction of the pillow top. If the pillow top has borders on which the finished width of the border is not crucial, use a ½" seam allowance for durability. If the pillow top is pieced so that a wider seam allowance would interfere with the design, use a ¼" seam allowance. Using the determined seam allowance (or stitching as close as possible to welting), sew pillow top and back together, leaving an opening at bottom edge for turning.
3. Turn pillow right side out, carefully pushing corners outward. Stuff with polyester fiberfill or pillow form and sew final closure by hand.

EMBROIDERY STITCHES
TRADITIONAL EMBROIDERY STITCHES

Blanket Stitch
Come up at 1. Go down at 2 and come up at 3, keeping thread below point of needle (**Fig. 65**). Continue working as shown in **Fig. 66**.

Fig. 65

Fig. 66

Feather Stitch
Come up at 1. Go down at 2 and come up at 3, keeping floss below point of needle (**Fig. 67**). Alternate stitches from right to left, keeping stitches symmetrical (**Fig. 68**).

Fig. 67

Fig. 68

French Knot
Come up at 1. Wrap thread once around needle and insert needle at 2, holding end of thread with non-stitching fingers (**Fig. 69**). Tighten knot; then pull needle through, holding floss until it must be released. For larger knot, use more strands; wrap only once.

Fig. 69

Herringbone Stitch
Coming up at odd numbers and going down at even numbers, work evenly spaced stitches as shown in **Fig. 70**.

Fig. 70

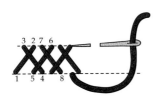

Lazy Daisy Stitch
Bring needle up at 1; take needle down again at 1 to form a loop and bring needle up at 2. Keeping loop below point of needle (**Fig. 71**), take needle down at 3 to anchor loop (**Fig. 72**).

Fig. 71

Fig. 72

Running Stitch
The running stitch consists of a series of straight stitches with the stitch length equal to the space between stitches (**Fig. 73**).

Fig. 73

Straight Stitch
Come up at 1 and go down at 2 (**Fig. 74**). Length of stitches may be varied as desired.

Fig. 74

Stem Stitch
Come up at 1. Keeping thread below the stitching line, go down at 2 and come up at 3. Go down at 4 and come up at 5 (**Fig. 75**).

Fig. 75

SILK RIBBON EMBROIDERY STITCHES
To retain the dimensional quality of silk ribbon, be careful not to pull it too tightly or twist it too much when stitching.

To thread needle, cut an approximate 14" length of ribbon. Thread 1 end of ribbon through eye of needle. Pierce same end of ribbon about 1/4" from end with point of needle (**Fig. 76**). Pull on remaining ribbon end, locking ribbon into eye of needle (**Fig. 77**).

Fig. 76   **Fig. 77**

To begin and end a length of ribbon, form a soft knot in ribbon by folding ribbon end about 1/4" and piercing needle through both layers (**Fig. 78**). Gently pull ribbon through to form a knot (**Fig. 79**). To end, secure ribbon on wrong side of fabric by tying a knot.

Fig. 78   **Fig. 79**

Couched Ribbon Bow
Cut a piece of ribbon desired length. Fold ribbon in half and mark fold. Sew ribbon to fabric at mark (**Fig. 80**). Tie ribbon into a bow. Arrange loops and streamers as desired and anchor with traditional embroidery French Knots (**Fig. 81**).

Fig. 80

Fig. 81

French Knot

Follow instructions for traditional embroidery **French Knot**, page 156, but wrap ribbon around needle twice (**Fig. 82**).

Fig. 82

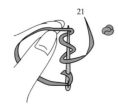

Japanese Ribbon Stitch

Bring needle up at 1. Lay ribbon flat on fabric and take needle down at 2, piercing ribbon (**Fig. 83**). Gently pull needle through to back. Ribbon will curl at end of stitch as shown in **Fig. 84**.

Fig. 83

Fig. 84

Lazy Daisy Stitch

Bring needle up at 1; take needle down again at 1 to form a loop and bring needle up at 2, allowing ribbon to twist and keeping ribbon below point of needle (**Fig. 85**). Take needle down at 3 to anchor loop.

Fig. 85

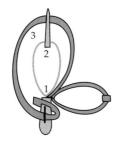

Loop Stitch

Bring needle up at 1. Use a large blunt needle or toothpick to hold ribbon flat on fabric. Take needle down at 2, using blunt needle to hold ribbon flat while pulling ribbon through to back of fabric (**Fig. 86**). Leave blunt needle in loop until needle is brought up at 3 for next loop (**Fig. 87**). Use embroidery floss to tack large loops in place.

Fig. 86

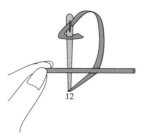

Fig. 87

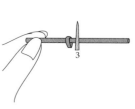

Spider Web Rose

Use a removable fabric marking pen to lightly draw a circle the desired size of rose. For anchor stitches, use 1 strand of embroidery floss to work 5 straight stitches from edge of circle to center, bringing needle up at odd numbers and taking needle down at even numbers (**Fig. 88**). For ribbon petals, bring needle up at center of anchor stitches; weave ribbon over and under anchor stitches (**Fig. 89**), keeping ribbon loose and allowing ribbon to twist. Continue to weave ribbon until anchor stitches are covered. Take needle down to wrong side of fabric.

Fig. 88

Fig. 89

Wrapped Straight Stitch

Begin with a straight stitch. Bring needle up again at 1. Keeping ribbon flat, wrap ribbon around stitch without catching fabric or stitch (**Fig. 90**). To end stitch, take needle down at 2 (**Fig. 91**).

Fig. 90

Fig. 91

GLOSSARY

Appliqué — A cut-out fabric shape that is secured to a larger background. Also refers to the technique of securing the cut-out pieces.

Backing — The back or bottom layer of a quilt, sometimes called the "lining."

Backstitch — A reinforcing stitch taken at the beginning and end of a seam to secure stitches.

Basting — Large running stitches used to temporarily secure pieces or layers of fabric together. Basting is removed after permanent stitching.

Batting — The middle layer of a quilt that provides the insulation and warmth as well as the thickness.

Bias — The diagonal (45° for true bias) grain of fabric in relation to crosswise or lengthwise grain (see **Fig. 92**).

Binding — The fabric strip used to enclose the raw edges of the layered and quilted quilt. Also refers to the technique of finishing quilt edges in this way.

Blindstitch — A method of hand sewing an opening closed so that it is invisible.

Border — Strips of fabric that are used to frame a quilt top.

Chain piecing — A machine-piecing method consisting of joining pairs of pieces one after the other by feeding them through the sewing machine without cutting the thread between the pairs.

Grain — The direction of the threads in woven fabric. "Crosswise grain" refers to the threads running from selvage to selvage. "Lengthwise grain" refers to the threads running parallel to the selvages (**Fig. 92**).

Fig. 92

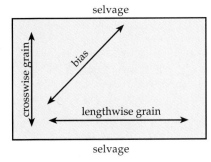

Machine baste — To baste using a sewing machine set at a long stitch length.

Miter — A method used to finish corners of quilt borders or bindings consisting of joining fabric pieces at a 45° angle.

Piecing — Sewing together the pieces of a quilt design to form a quilt block or an entire quilt top.

Pin basting — Using rustproof safety pins to secure the layers of a quilt together prior to machine quilting.

Quilt blocks — Pieced or appliquéd sections that are sewn together to form a quilt top.

Quilt top — The decorative part of a quilt that is layered on top of the batting and backing.

Quilting — The stitching that holds together the 3 quilt layers (top, batting, and backing); or, the entire process of making a quilt.

Sashing — Strips or blocks of fabric that separate individual blocks in a quilt top.

Seam allowance — The distance between the seam and the cut edge of the fabric. In quilting, the seam allowance is usually ¼".

Selvages — The 2 finished lengthwise edges of fabric (see **Fig. 92**). Selvages should be trimmed from fabric before cutting.

Set (or Setting) — The arrangement of the quilt blocks as they are sewn together to form the quilt top.

Setting squares — Squares of plain (unpieced) fabric set between pieced or appliquéd quilt blocks in a quilt top.

Setting triangles — Triangles of fabric used around the outside of a diagonally set quilt top to fill in between outer squares and border or binding.

Stencil — A pattern used for marking quilting lines.

Straight grain — The crosswise or lengthwise grain of fabric (see **Fig. 92**). The lengthwise grain has the least amount of stretch.

Strip set — Two or more strips of fabric that are sewn together along the long edges and then cut apart across the width of the sewn strips to create smaller units.

Template — A pattern used for marking quilt pieces to be cut out.

Triangle-square — In piecing, 2 right triangles joined along their long sides to form a square with a diagonal seam (**Fig. 93**).

Fig. 93

Unit — A pieced section that is made as individual steps in the quilt construction process are completed. Units are usually combined to make blocks or other sections of the quilt top.

CREDITS

We want to extend a warm *thank you* to the generous people who allowed us to photograph our projects at their homes.

- *Ruffled Wedding Ring Collection*:
  Bill and Nancy Appleton
- *So-Easy String Jacket*: Mike and Jodie Davis
- *Stylish Cake Stand Collection*:
  Jim and Joan Adams
- *Hidden Stars Collection:* Tom and Robin Steves
- *Building Blocks*: John and Jane Prather
- *Heartwarming Wall Hangings*:
  John and Jane Prather
- *Endless Stars*: Duncan and Nancy Porter
- *Churn Dash Maze:* Bob and Donna Roten
- *Crazy About Blue Collection*:
  Dr. Dan and Sandra Cook
- *Hourglasses & Geese:* Bob and Donna Roten
- *Jacob's Ladder Collection*:
  Bill and Nancy Appleton
- *Baby Blue Collection:* Susan and Brian Bell
- *Dutch Windmill:* John and Jane Prather
- *Oak and Laurel Collection:*
  Carl and Monte Brunck

We wish to thank The Empress of Little Rock Bed and Breakfast, Little Rock, Arkansas, for allowing us to photograph our Lost Ships and Good Fortune collections at the inn.

We also thank Linens 'N Things of Little Rock, Arkansas, for the use of the bedding accessories that appear on pages 40-43; The Heights Toy Center, Little Rock, Arkansas, for the use of the toy sailboats that appear on page 104; and Young @ Art, Little Rock, Arkansas, for the use of the embroidered pillows that appear on page 105.

Special thanks go to Tom and Robin Steves for the use of their cat, Hardy, which appears on page 41.

The following projects were designed by Sharon LoMonaco: the Double Wedding Ring quilt, pillow shams, throw pillow, and valance, pages 8-11, and the Building Blocks quilt, pages 48-49.

Thanks also go to Viking Husqvarna Sewing Machine Company of Cleveland, Ohio, for providing the sewing machines used to make many of the projects in this book.

To Magna IV Color Imaging of Little Rock, Arkansas, we say thank you for the superb color reproduction and excellent pre-press preparation.

We especially want to thank photographers Mark Mathews, Larry Pennington, Karen Shirey, and Ken West of Peerless Photography, Little Rock, Arkansas, and Jerry R. Davis of Jerry Davis Photography, Little Rock, Arkansas, for their time, patience, and excellent work.

We extend a sincere *thank you* to all the people who assisted in making and testing the projects in this book: Karen Call, Wanda Fite, Judith Hassed, Barbara Middleton, Ruby Solida, Glenda Taylor, Karen Tyler, and the Gardner Memorial United Methodist Church Quilters, North Little Rock, Arkansas: Elois Allain, Vina Lindermon, Fredda McBride, Betty Smith, Esther Starkey, Maxine Bramblett, Leon Dickey, and Grace Brooks.